Vera
Lex

Journal of the International Natural Law Society

New Series Volume 5, Numbers 1&2   Winter 2004

COPYRIGHT © 2004
PACE UNIVERSITY PRESS
1 PACE PLAZA
NEW YORK, NY 10038

ISBN 0-944473-70-9
ISSN 0893-4851

CONTRIBUTORS
Address all submissions and correspondence to The Editor, VERA LEX, Pace University, Department of Philosophy & Religious Studies, 1 Pace Plaza, New York, NY 10038. Please send two copies of the paper submitted. Include adequate margins, double space everything (text, notes, works cited, quotations). Use U.S. spelling and punctuation style, (e.g. periods inside quotation marks; "double quotes" for opening and closing quotations). The University of Chicago Manual of Style, 13th Edition, is to be consulted regarding matters of style. Notes are to be numbered consecutively (in Arabic numerals) and placed at the bottom of the page.

SUBSCRIBERS
VERA LEX is published annually by Pace University Press, 41 Park Row, Room 1510, New York, NY 10038. Subscription price: $40. Please send all subscription inquiries to: PaceUP@services.pace.edu

INDEXING AND ABSTRACTING
VERA LEX is indexed in *Philosopher's Index*.

VERA LEX, the journal of the International Natural Law Society, was established to communicate and dialogue on the subject of natural law and natural right, to introduce natural law philosophy into the mainstream of contemporary thought, and to strengthen the current revived interest in the discussion of morals and law and advance its historical research.

Why do we use a shell (*Nautilus pomplilus Linnaeus*) to symbolize *vera lex*? The logarithmic spiraling and overlapping chambers of the shell are endless. They suggest a patterned development and evolution that, by its radial and circular design, never comes to an end. This means that the shell is at once specific and real, while its form, like law, is abstract and ideal.

The pattern of a shell is, like good law, uniform, regular and reliable. It can therefore be anticipated and known. The pattern of a shell is balanced, like justice. *Una iustitia.*

A shell is a biological being. Like law, it has life and dynamic. It grows. (There is an average of thirty growth lines per chamber, one for every day in the lunar cycle, suggesting that a new chamber is put down each lunar month and a new growth line each day, thus recording two different natural rhythms, lunar and solar.)

The shell is a universal and common object known to everyone. A shell is not soft tissue easily destroyed. And yet, like liberty, it is fragile in certain respects if stepped on with an iron boot. It has to be guarded with vigilance or it is crushed.

In every shell lives a nautilus. If the shell is law, the nautilus (snail) is a person—it is alive—person and law. Their destinies, like person and law, are interdependent.

Vera Lex

leges innumerae, una iustitia

CONTENTS

NEW SERIES VOLUME 5, NUMBERS 1 & 2　　　　　　　WINTER 2004

EDITOR'S NOTE

As you will notice, we changed the format of *Vera Lex* for this issue. We decided to forgo the annotated bibliography. An annotated bibliography on the topic of medieval natural law would require volumes and still come up short, while focusing specifically on articles in this volume would be redundant since the individual citations will suffice.

Also, you will notice the paucity of book reviews, a valuable feature for the broad dissemination of recent scholarship. We moved our offices over the summer and have been operating from makeshift facilities (a scattered array of cartons, some correctly labeled). You have my personal apology and promise of publication in a future issue.

The present volume dedicated to medieval natural law is a testament to the enduring importance of the topic, but, mostly, to the diligent efforts of Professor Mark Gossiaux who collected a wonderful series of articles sure to advance medieval natural law scholarship. I am grateful for his learned and insightful selection along with his scrupulous editorial skills.

GUEST EDITORIAL

It is widely acknowledged that medieval thinkers made many important contributions to the history of philosophy. Gone are the days in which the history of philosophy is said to have begun with Plato and Aristotle, and then passed uneventfully to Descartes. The Middle Ages, that long period from the fall of Rome (476) to the capture of Constantinople by the Turks (1453), has in the twentieth century become a field of intense scholarly study. Medieval thinkers have been recognized for their important work in philosophical theology and metaphysics; today an increasing number of analytically trained scholars are studying medieval logic and semantic theory. Medieval Latin philosophers are also notable for their contributions to the history of natural law. Perhaps the best known proponent of natural law in the Middle Ages was Thomas Aquinas. Although his discussion of natural law occupies only a few pages of his vast corpus of writings, it is one of the best-known parts of his philosophy. Yet Aquinas is not merely a historical figure; he continues to inspire contemporary natural law theorists. Two of the leading proponents of natural law, Germain Grisez and John Finnis, have claimed that their own work is a recovery of the natural law theory of Thomas Aquinas. For those who wish to follow contemporary discussions of natural law, the study of the medievals is not without value.

The essays in the present volume explore various aspects of medieval natural law theory. In the first essay James M. Jacobs ("The Transcendentals and the Precepts of the Natural Law") examines how Thomas Aquinas' natural law ethics has its foundation in his understanding of the transcendentals. The latter are those concepts (such as true, good, and one) which are coextensive with the concept of being. Making use of the connection between being and goodness, Jacobs offers a corrective to the anti-metaphysical approach to natural law adopted by Grisez and Finnis, by showing how the transcendentals are involved in Thomas' derivation of natural law precepts.

In a very provocative essay, Peter A. Redpath ("Why Double Effect and Proportionality are not Moral Principles for St. Thomas") challenges the assumption of many scholars that Thomas' ethics is merely a natural law ethics. To correct this misunderstanding he makes an analysis of Thomas' teaching on the subject of a science. Redpath concedes that notions such as double effect and proportionality are used by Aquinas, but he rejects the claim that they enjoy the status of moral principles in his thought. Other notions, such as the concept of justice, are more primary.

Mark D. Gossiaux ("Thomas Aquinas on our Natural Desire for a Supernatural End") examines a puzzle concerning Thomas Aquinas' teaching on happiness. Thomas affirms that all human beings have a natural desire for happiness, and that the ultimate end of human life is to see God as he is in himself. One might wonder whether this end is a natural one, or whether it is merely supernatural. Thomas' texts seem to yield conflicting answers: sometimes he affirms that the vision of God is man's end; at other times he denies this, since man cannot attain this vision through his own efforts. Thomas himself is unaware of any apparent contradiction in his teaching. In reviewing Thomas' texts on happiness, Gossiaux argues that Thomas' views on faith and reason control his teaching on happiness: philosophical analysis can show that human happiness is found only in the vision of God, yet for the philosopher this knowledge remains vague and indistinct, requiring to be completed by the testimony of faith.

Polycarp Ikuenobe ("Descriptive Procedural Aspects of Aquinas's Natural Law Theory") examines one of the central criticisms of Thomas Aquinas made by legal positivists, namely, that he has confused the problem of the validity of a law (i.e., whether it satisfies the identity conditions required of all laws) with that of its moral adequacy (i.e., whether it is just or not). What provokes the ire of the positivists is Thomas' statement that an unjust law is not a law. Ikuenobe argues that the positivist criticism is misplaced, since Aquinas' theory of law contains both a descriptive procedural account of the nature of law and a substantive content account. The fact that a law is substantively just is neither a necessary nor sufficient condition for its legal validity.

Stephen Rowntree S.J. ("Aquinas' Economic Ethics: Profoundly Anticapitalistic?") looks at an important, albeit often neglected, aspect of Aquinas' social thought. Some have charged that Aquinas' view of economics is anticapitalistic, because of his theory of a "just price" and his rejection of usury. The former is thought to imply that the value of a good is determined not by market conditions of supply and demand but rather by its intrinsic value; this would seem to rule out the notion of buying and selling for profit. The latter appears to conflict with the principles of the modern banking system, and would rule out all investment for profit. Rowntree argues, however, that Aquinas finds nothing intrinsically wrong with such activities. What Thomas offers is rather a business ethics, or the outlines for a moral capitalism.

The essays in the present volume should stimulate further reflection on the nature of medieval natural law theory. An awareness of this tradition is important not merely for the historian, but also for the contemporary theorist, whose thinking cannot fail to be enriched by a contact with these sources.

FEATURED ARTICLES

THE TRANSCENDENTALS AND THE PRECEPTS OF THE NATURAL LAW

James M. Jacobs

I suppose that one might consider this paper another skirmish in the long battle over the anti-metaphysical approach to natural law theory first suggested by Germain Grisez.[1] However, since there have already been many persuasive responses to that theory,[2] I hope to address a more specific issue related to the dependence of natural law on metaphysics in the thought of Thomas Aquinas. The essence of the responses to the new natural law theory typically is to ground the natural law on the Aristotelian metaphysics of substantial form, act, and potency.[3] I believe, though, that this interpretation overlooks the foundational insights of Thomistic metaphysics as focused not simply on essence, but on *esse*, existence. It is being or existence that is the universal foundation of all that is.[4]

---

[1] See Germain Grisez, "The First Principle of Practical Reason: A Commentary on the *Summa Theologia*, 1-2, Question 94, Article 2," *Natural Law Forum* 10 (1965): 168-201; and John Finnis, *Natural Law and Natural Right* (Oxford: Clarendon, 1980).

[2] Three representative examples are Janice Schultz, "Thomistic Metaethics and a Present Controversy," *Thomist* 52 (1988): 40-62; Peter Simpson, "Practical Knowing: Finnis and Aquinas," *Modern Schoolman* 67 (1990): 111-122; and Lawrence Dewan, "St. Thomas, Natural Lights, and the Moral Order," *Angelicum* 67 (1990): 285-308. Dewan clearly points out that metaphysics sets the *starting point* for ethical reflection in Thomas and so is presupposed by the entire ethical project.

[3] See, for example, Anthony J. Lisska, *Aquinas's Theory of Natural Law: An Analytic Reconstruction* (Oxford: Clarendon Press, 1996). On page 124, Lisska sums up his view of natural law's reliance upon metaphysics in strictly Aristotelian terms in this way: "The natural law, in the mind of Aquinas, is nothing more than the determination of the ends—read final cause—of the dispositional properties of the essence—read formal cause—of the human person."

[4] See Etienne Gilson, *Being and Some Philosophers.* Second edition. (Toronto: Pontifical Institute of Medieval Studies, 1952), 154-189; and, *The Christian Philosophy of St. Thomas Aquinas.* Translated by L.K. Shook, C.S.B. (Notre Dame: University of Notre Dame Press, 1994), 29-54.

Moreover, in light of the convertibility of being with other transcendental properties, Thomas recognizes that being is also the foundation for his metaphysics of the good. That transcendental convertibility is, therefore, crucial for his ethics. As Jan Aertsen has said, "Metaphysics and ethics are joined together and connected at a philosophical level by the doctrine of the transcendentals. They appear to have a founding function: the first principle of theoretical reason is reduced to the first truth, being; the first principle of practical reason to the good."[5] In this paper I will explore how Thomistic ethics is founded on the transcendentals; in particular, I will argue that the order of the precepts of the natural can be understood only when viewed in terms of their transcendental foundation. There will be two main sections to this discussion. The first section will introduce the convertibility of being and goodness, and will discuss some pertinent consequences; the second section will be a close reading of the critical test, *Summa Theologica* I-II.94.2, in light of what I have established about the transcendentals.

BEING AND GOODNESS

The transcendental properties, for Thomas, are those properties which belong to every being because it exists, regardless of what mode of existence it might have. In other words, the transcendental properties transcend the categorical divisions of being which characterize the Aristotelian substance-accident distinction. Thus, any property that is common to all substances and accidents is a transcendental.[6]

The foundation of the transcendentals is being, for necessarily there is nothing that exists outside of being; not-being does not exist. *Being* transcends the subject/accident distinction, for every actual substance and real accident has being. But the source and cause of this universal property is the act of existence, for it is the act of existence, which makes everything actual: "Existence is the most perfect of all things, for it is

---

[5] Aertsen, *Medieval Philosophy and the Transcendental: The Case of Thomas Aquinas*, Studien und Texte zur Geistesgeschichte des Mittelalters 52 (Leyden/New York/Cologne: Brill, 1996), p. 330.

[6] For Thomas's derivation of the transcendentals, see *De Veritate* 1.1 and 21.1, from which I draw below. Citations from *De Veritate* are taken from *Truth*, 3 vols., tr. by Robert W. Mulligan, S.J., James V. McGlynn, S.J., and Robert W. Schmidt, S.J. (Chicago: Henry Regnery, 1954; reprint, Indianapolis: Hackett, 1994).

compared to all things as that by which they are made actual; for nothing has actuality except insofar as it exists. Hence existence is that which actuates all things, even their forms."[7] Moreover, the act of existence is what actualizes the proper activities of each nature, the operations by which a creature is perfected in fully actualizing the potency inherent in its nature: "Wherefore it is clear that *being* as we understand it here is the actuality of all acts, and therefore the perfection of all perfections."[8] Being as the act of existence is therefore the most universal cause that unites disparate entities together under one general explanatory form, being as the transcendental fact of existence.

Since nothing exists outside of being, the other transcendental properties cannot be something other than being. Thomas says, therefore, that they are conceptual additions to being; that is, they are *being* as considered under a certain aspect. Since every entity necessarily is a being, every entity will also have each of these conceptual properties. Two of these transcendental properties are aspects of being which become evident whenever a being is understood in relation to a soul: insofar as a soul has an intellectual power, a being can be understood as *true*; insofar as the soul has an appetitive power, a being can be desired as *good*. In this way, being becomes the metaphysical touchstone for operations of the soul. As such, it will also ground the first principles by which the soul is inclined to its proper operations of knowing and willing.

It is in explicating the transcendentals and showing how the good is simply being under the aspect of desirability that Thomas gives his most fundamental characterization of good.[9] It is this characterization that will ultimately define all kinds of goodness, including moral goodness. Thomas clarifies this broad notion of goodness by arguing that the good is being as actualized or perfected:

[7] *Summa Theologica* I.4.1.ad 3. (Henceforth, *ST*. All references to this work are to the translation by the Fathers of the English Dominican Province (New York: Benzinger, 1948; reprint, Allen, TX: Christian Classics, 1981.))

[8] *De Potentia* 7.2.ad 9. Citations are to *On the Power of God (*Quaestiones Disputatae de Potentia Dei), 3 vols., tr. by the English Dominican Fathers (London: Burns Oates & Washbourne, 1933).

[9] Of course, Thomas also defines *good* in his analysis of God, who, as the necessary extrinsic cause of being, is the supereminent cause of all transcendental properties; see *ST* I.6.

> Goodness and being are really the same, and differ only in idea; which is clear from the following arguments. The essence of goodness consists in this, that it is in some way desirable. Hence the Philosopher says: *Goodness is what all desire.* Now it is clear that a thing is desirable only in so far as it is perfect; for all desire their own perfection. But everything is perfect so far as it is actual. Therefore it is clear that a thing is perfect so far as it exists; for it is existence that makes all things actual. Hence it is clear that goodness and being are the same really. But goodness presents the aspect of desirableness, which being does not present.[10]

Now, while all beings are good inasmuch as they are the perfection of the passive potentiality of matter to become a substance,[11] the true denotation of the *good* is the perfection of being, that is, the perfection of a substance in terms of its proper operations. Every substance is naturally inclined to this as the perfection of its specific nature.[12] Indeed, as Thomas repeatedly argues, every substance acts according as it is in act;[13] more than this, though, each thing exists entirely for the sake of its perfective operation.[14] What is critical in this assertion is what underlies this inherent dynamism: it is the act of existence that, *as act*, ultimately motivates this inclination to perfection. It is this same act of existence that is

[10] *ST* I.5.1.c.

[11] See *De Principiis Naturae* c. 1; this is goodness *secundum quid*, as Thomas points out in *ST* I.5.1.ad 1.

[12] See *De Veritate* 1.10. ad 3, contrary difficulties: "There are two kinds of perfection, first and second. First perfection is the form of each thing, and that by which it has its act of existing. Nothing is without it while it continues in existence. Second perfection is operation, which is the end of a thing or the means by which a thing reaches its end; and a thing is sometimes deprived of this perfection. The note of truth in things results from first perfection; for it is because a thing has a form that it imitates the art of the divine intellect and produces knowledge of itself in the soul. But the note of goodness in a thing results from its second perfection, for this goodness arises from the end."

[13] See, e.g., *Summa Contra Gentiles* II.1.1 (hereafter *SCG*.) Cf. *SCG* III.97.4, I.28.7, II.67.7. References to *SCG* are to the four volumes translation by Anton Pegis, James Anderson, and Vernon Bourke (Notre Dame, IN: University of Notre Dame Press, 1975).

[14] See *ST* I.105.5.c.: "For the less perfect is always for the sake of the more perfect: and consequently as the matter is for the sake of the form, so the form which is the first act, is for the sake of its operation, which is the second act; and thus operation is the end of the creature." See also *SCG* I.43.2 and III.113.1.

the transcendental ground of all that is. Therefore, while all beings naturally have an inclination to perfection because of their status as actual (in
act), each species will have, according to its mode of existence, unique
operations by which it is perfected. In other words, by virtue of its participation in the act of existence, all being is by nature active, and that
activity is for the perfection of being. This is the purpose of activity as
flowing out of substantial being. As Thomas says, "Now, the very fact of
being is a good, and so all things desire to be. Therefore, every action and
movement are for the sake of a good. Moreover, every action and movement are for the sake of some perfection."[15] Consequently, because all
being is by nature dynamic, the inclination to goodness is an inherent universal property of being that is manifested in every activity by which two
substances are brought into relation.

It is this fact of the act of existence simultaneously underlying both
the stability of substantial form and the dynamism of proper operations
that allows us to explain how the transcendental properties furnish the
first principles of speculative and practical reason. The speculative intellect is that use of the intellect by which truth is obtained.[16] Since truth is
the adequation of the mind and being,[17] every recognition of truth is simply a recognition of some determinate act of existence, or form. As
Thomas says, "Everything is knowable insofar as it is in act, and not insofar as it is in potentiality: for a thing is a being, and is true, and therefore
knowable, according as it is actual."[18] Now, while grasping particular
forms can ground first principles for specific sciences, no one form can
establish the very first principle common to all sciences; the only thing
that can ground that first principle is our recognition of transcendental
being—the act of existence as the universal nonspecific intrinsic cause.
This, then, yields the first principle of speculative reason: nothing can be
and not be simultaneously. This, in turn, grounds the most fundamental
conclusion of the convertibility between being and truth; no proposition
can be simultaneously affirmed and denied.

[15] *SCG* III.3.4-5.
[16] *ST* I.79.11.c.
[17] *De Veritate* 1.1.c.
[18] *ST* I.87.1.c.

Practical reason is continuous with speculative reason for, as Thomas says, they are not distinct powers, but rather speculative reason is made practical by extension.[19] Since speculative reason grasps the act of existence in terms of a formal nature, practical reason grasps the dynamic tendency of that nature's act of existence to the good. Practical reason is directed to the determination of actions by which the agent is to be perfected. Thus, the practical intellect is that use of the intellect by which man determines which activities offered for consideration by the speculative intellect are most worthy of pursuit because they are perfective of human nature. Just as the first principle of speculative reason has to ground all sciences, so the first principle of practical reason has to recognize the universal characteristic of action: all activity is for the sake of the good. Thus, while the first principle of speculative reason is based on the stability of the first act of being (something either is or is not), the first principle of practical reason is based on the dynamism of being to perfection and the contingent possession of that second act. Therefore, the first practical principle is: the good is to be done.

One consequence of practical reason merely extending speculative reason is that it makes it necessary that the principle of practical reason rely on the principle of speculative reason. Both first principles, therefore, assume the grasp of being as the dynamic act of existence as the most universal intrinsic cause. Moreover, in order to know more specific precepts of practical reason, we must know how that act of existence is specified to a nature, for it is in knowing the nature of an agent that we can grasp the operations most appropriate for that agent. Thus, we first apprehend the truth of being and only then we can understand its inclination to perfection.[20]

It is clear that the first principles of speculative reason and practical reason are defined in terms of the transcendental properties of truth and goodness inasmuch as they are convertible with being. It is also clear that there is a dependence of the principle of practical reason upon speculative

[19] *ST* I.79.11. *sed contra.*

[20] See *ST* I.16.4.ad 2: "Now the intellect apprehends primarily being itself; secondly, it apprehends that it understands being; and thirdly, it apprehends that it desires being. Hence the idea of being is first, that of truth second, and the idea of good third, though good is in things."

reason. These insights are operative in Thomas's treatment of the precepts of the natural law in *Summa Theologica*, I-II.94.2. This dependence must therefore be recognized in order to understand the real foundation of natural law. Let us now turn to that important text.

SUMMA THEOLOGICA I-II.94.2

Throughout the discussion of Question 94, Thomas makes clear that there are a variety of precepts involved in knowing the natural law. I will argue that the distinction between these precepts is intimately bound up with the foundational notion of the transcendentals because Thomas's most basic understanding of goodness is in terms of its convertibility with being. I hope to demonstrate that those precepts that are based directly on the transcendentals are self-evident to all; other precepts are more specific and less self-evident based on their relationship to this very first precept. I will elaborate on this by means of a close reason of the critical text of the *Prima Secundae*, the second article of Question 94.

Natural law is defined as a rational creature's participation in the eternal law;[21] that is, the natural law is man's practical understanding of the providential ordering of human nature to its proper end. As mentioned above, Thomas says that by nature all things are inclined to their end; but humans, by virtue of our rational nature, are inclined to that end in two ways:[22] we are passively directed to our perfection by the Eternal Law, as all creatures are; but we also have an active share in providence insofar as we are rational and can voluntarily direct our actions to perfection.[23] It is because of this twofold participation in the eternal law that there are two rules or measures of human activity: reason is the proximate rule, while the eternal law is the ultimate rule since it alone establishes our inclinations to perfection.[24] It is with respect to this rational participation that reason requires the recognition of first principles, for without

[21] *ST* I-II.91.2.c.

[22] *ST* I-II.91.2.c.

[23] The first may be understood as being founded on our participation in the act of existence which inclines us by nature to perfection; the second can be seen as our participation in divine reason itself, since knowledge of truth is "a reflection of and participation in the eternal law" (*ST* I-II.93.2).

[24] *ST* I-II.21.1.c. and I-II.71.6.c.

them we would not be inclined to a rational grasp of our capacity for perfection at all.[25] Upon these first principles are based all other more specific precepts of practical reason which lead us to natural perfection.[26]
Thomas introduces his discussion of the precepts of the natural law in
three sections. First, he examines the nature of self-evidence; then, he discusses the first precept of practical reason; finally, he lists the other self-
evident precepts. My discussion will follow that order.

Self-Evidence and the Transcendentals. Thomas begins *Summa
Theologica* I-II.94.2 by stating the need for self-evident principles:

> As stated above, the precepts of the natural law are to the prac-
> tical reason, what the first principles of demonstrations are to
> the speculative reason; because both are self-evident princi-
> ples. Now a thing is said to be self-evident in two ways: first,
> in itself; secondly, in relation to us. Any proposition is said to
> be self-evident in itself, if its predicate is contained in the
> notion of the subject: although, to one who knows not the def-
> inition of the subject, it happens that such a proposition is not
> self-evident. For instance, this proposition, *Man is a rational
> being*, is, in its very nature, self-evident, since who says *man*,
> says *a rational being*: and yet to one who knows not what a
> man is, this proposition is not self-evident. Hence it is that, as
> Boethius says, certain axioms or propositions are universally
> self-evident to all; and such are those propositions whose terms
> are known to all, as *Every whole is greater than its part*, and,
> *Things equal to one and the same are equal to one another*.
> But some propositions are self-evident only to the wise, who
> understand the meaning of the terms of such propositions: thus
> to one who understands that an angel is not a body, it is self-
> evident that an angel is not circumscriptively in a place: but
> this is not evident to the unlearned, for they cannot grasp it.

[25] See *De Veritate* 14.2.c.: "Nothing can be directed to any end unless there pre-exists
in it a certain proportion to the end, and it is from this that the desire of the end arises in
it.... This is why there is in human nature a certain initial participation of the good which
is proportionate to that nature. For self-evident principles of demonstration, which are
seeds of the contemplation of wisdom, naturally pre-exist in that good, as do principles of
natural law, which are seeds of the moral virtues."

[26] See *De Veritate* 10.6.c.: "And in this way all knowledge is in a certain sense implant-
ed in us from the beginning (since we have the light of the agent intellect) through the
medium of universal conceptions which are immediately known by the light of the agent
intellect. These serve as universal principles through which we judge about other things,
and in which we foreknow these others."

Thomas begins this passage by noting that there are two kinds of self-evident propositions: propositions that are self-evident in themselves and those that are self-evident to all.[27] A clear statement of the significance of this distinction comes from the article on whether God's existence is self-evident: "If, therefore the essence of the predicate and subject be known to all, the proposition will be self-evident to all; as is clear with regard to the first principles of demonstration, the terms of which are common things that no one is ignorant of, such as being and non-being, whole and part, and such like. If, however, there are some to whom the essence of the predicate and subject is unknown, the proposition will be self-evident in itself, but not to those who do not know the meaning of the predicate and subject of the proposition."[28] The key insight of this distinction lies in the degree of evidentness with respect to the essence in question. The nature of truly universal, or common, essences will be self-evident to all; those that require knowledge of a specific nature are self-evident in themselves, but not to all.

Now, since all knowledge comes from sense-experience,[29] only those essences which are universally experienced can be said to be self-evident to all. It seems unlikely, then, given the contingency of experience and the difficulty of knowing substantial forms,[30] that knowledge of any specific nature would be self-evident to all. Thomas asserts, though, that there must be some essences that are evident to all; these principles must be constitutive of all being, not just specific natures. I would argue that these most fundamental principles must be based on the transcendentals, for they are based on the fact that being is the most universal property and, therefore, first in the intellect. Because being is first in the intellect, the first principle of all speculative reasoning is the self-evident truth that

---

[27] He makes this distinction many times when discussing self-evidence: for example, *An Exposition of the 'On the Hebdomads' of Boethius* , Ch.1; *De Veritate* 10.12.c.; *Commentary on Aristotle's "Metaphysics"* IV.5; *Commentary on the "Posterior analytics" of Aristotle* I.5.

[28] *ST* I.2.1.c.

[29] See *De Veritate* 16.1.c., where Thomas says that man's self-evident knowledge, unlike that of angels, must be derived from sense-experience.

[30] See *ST* I.77.ad 7.

something either is or is not.[31] This is the basis of all intellectual judgment, for all judgment is about *what is*; accordingly, all knowledge follows from this principle. Furthermore, since being is convertible with the other transcendental properties, there are self-evident notions regarding being as understood under each aspect. Thus, as *one*, being self-evidently yields the whole-part distinction; as *true*, it is evident that the same proposition cannot be simultaneously affirmed and denied; and, as we shall see, as *good* it is self-evident that the natural dynamism of being to action is for the sake of perfection and so is to be pursued. As integral to any and all experience of being, these principles are the true first principles upon which all demonstration and knowledge will be based.

It is clear, therefore, how propositions that are self-evident to all differ from those which are self-evident in themselves but not to all: the former are founded on the transcendental properties which are always present to experience, while the latter require contingent knowledge of a specific nature. It follows, then, that if one knows the essence of a specific nature in question, then one can know the properties that are necessarily inherent in that nature. But the critical point is that someone can be ignorant of this since the knowledge of any specific nature is not such that it permeates all experience by necessity. Hence, these truths are only self-evident in themselves, but not to all. Nevertheless, the principles derived from knowledge of a specific nature are still self-evident, for with each determinate mode of existence come necessary properties; for example, if this is a man, then it follows necessarily that he is rational.[32] In this way, a delimited mode of being yields delimited principles of knowledge.

The First Precept of Practical Reason. We now turn to the first principle of practical reason, that which is self-evident to all on the basis of the transcendental notion of the good. We can then demonstrate how

---

31 See *Commentary on Aristotle's "Metaphysics"* IV.6.600-610 for Thomas's discussion of this.

32 To put this another way, the principles that are self-evident to all are the truly common principles of all knowledge while the principles that are self-evident in themselves but not to all are the proper principles for any given subject. Compare this to the idea that while everyone knows these first principles, the knowledge of any particular science requires special knowledge of a nature; see *Commentary on the "Posterior analytics" of Aristotle* I.18-20.

moral precepts of specifically human goodness are based upon this principle. Let us first look at the second section of 94.2:

> Now a certain order is to be found in things that are apprehended universally. For that which, before aught else, falls under apprehension, is *being*, the notion of which is included in all things whatsoever a man apprehends. Wherefore the first indemonstrable principle is that *the same thing cannot be affirmed and denied at the same time*, which is based on the notion of *being* and *not being*: and on this principle all others are based, as is stated in *Metaph.* IV.9. Now as *being* is the first thing that falls under apprehension simply, so *good* is the first thing that falls under the apprehension of the practical reason, which is directed to action: since every agent acts for an end under the aspect of good. Consequently the first principle in the practical reason is one founded on the notion of good, viz., that *good is that which all things seek after.* Hence this is the first precept of law, that *good is to be done and pursued, and evil is to be avoided.* All other precepts of the natural law are based upon this: so that whatever the practical reason naturally apprehends as man's good (or evil) belongs to the precepts of the natural law as something to be done or avoided.

In this passage, Thomas makes three general points. First, he argues that there is a certain order among the self-evident principles. Second, he specifies that the first principles of speculative reason and practical reason are founded on the two transcendentals: being and good.[33] Third, he states he distinguishes this principle from the first precept of natural law, and claims that other precepts of natural law are based upon this first transcendental principle of practical reason.

Thomas first argues that there is a certain order among the self-evident principles, an order which manifests the dependence of the good upon being. That is, what is first recognized is the fact of being as the most common property; then, in recognizing that every being exists for the sake of its operation and so is by nature dynamically inclined to perfection, it is evident that being by nature acts for an end. But the end for

---

[33] That it is transcendental being and good is made evident by the fact that (1) the principle obtains for all entities and (2) that this is the *first* principle which must be common for all types of activity.

which all things act is the good; thus, this is a transcendental notion of the good, one that transcends all differences and encompasses all natures' potency to perfection. This undifferentiated end of activity in general is articulated in the first principle of practical reason: "good is that which all things seek after." This is self-evident because being itself (first actuality) involves the natural dynamism to perfection (second actuality) inherent in the act of existence.

Based on this understanding of the first principle, Thomas can then state the first *precept* of the natural law. Thomas says that law is a directive of practical reason that acts as a rule or measure; the metaphysical principle or fact that all things seek after the good becomes a precept of the natural law when practical reason posits it as a rule or measure for actions to be undertaken. It is in this way that practical reason extends speculative reason's grasp of the mode of existence and turns it to a measure of the goodness of action. The first directive measure of practical action is, therefore, a rule that simply prescribes the obvious, given the general principle of all practical reason: "good is to be done and pursued, and evil is to be avoided." All action is to be measured according to whether it has achieved what all action naturally aims at: the perfection of being. This law reflects the universal principle of action; hence, it is formal and empty of substantive content. This formality reflects the fact that it is based on the transcendental properties: it is founded upon the transcendental notion of goodness as the desirability of perfection inherent in all being as dynamic. Nevertheless, just as the principle of speculative reason needs to be supplemented by rules for the various sciences, this first law must be augmented by further precepts which guide behavior in a more specific way according to the nature of the agent in question.[34]

Other Self-Evident Precepts of the Natural Law. From the first (purely formal and transcendental) principle, more specific precepts regarding the good of determinate natures can be discovered. This is because being is received according to determinate modes or natures; consequently, there is a specific goodness for each nature. Hence, every being must act according to its nature for the perfection of its nature. Therefore, in any

---

[34] Of course, only rational creatures are at issue here, since they alone participate in the eternal law in a twofold manner: by passive inclination and by the active rule of reason.

human act generated from our rational nature, man can rationally discern those goods appropriate for human nature. These precepts are self-evident, but only in themselves and not to all. Recall that Thomas explicitly said at the beginning of 94.2 that "man is a rational animal" is not self-evident to all; that is so because any specific form requires contingent knowledge of that nature and that nature's proper end. Nevertheless, these precepts are not derived: they are immediately evident given the nature of the agent, since action follows from being. They do, however, require a cognizance of what humans are about in the world, a cognizance that in inherent in every human act, but excluded with respect to acts of man. So, while they are self-evident, people do not necessarily consciously recognize them as goods at all times, since not all actions arise out of knowledge and freedom. However, to the extent they do arise out of reason, they ought to be rational and in accordance with the natural law. Thomas argues for the determination of these self-evident precepts in the third section of 94.2:

> Since, however, good has the nature of an end, and evil, the nature of the contrary, hence it is that all those things to which man has a natural inclination, are naturally apprehended by reason as being good, and consequently as objects of pursuit, and their contraries as evil, and objects of avoidance. Wherefore according to the order of natural inclinations, is the order of the precepts of the natural law. Because in man there is first of all an inclination to good in accordance with the nature which he has in common with all substances: inasmuch as every substance seeks the preservation of its own being, according to its nature: and by reason of this inclination, whatever is a means of preserving human life, and of warding off its obstacles, belongs to the natural law. Secondly, there is in man an inclination to things that pertain to him more specially, *according to that nature which he has in common with other animals*: and in virtue of this inclination, those things are said to belong to the natural law, which nature has taught to all animals, such as sexual intercourse, education of offspring and so forth. Thirdly, there is in man an inclination to good, according to the nature of his reason, which nature is proper to him: thus man has a natural inclination to know the truth about God, and to live in society: and in this respect, whatever pertains to

> this inclination belongs to the natural law; for instance, to shun
> ignorance, to avoid offending those among whom one has to
> live, and other such things regarding the above inclination.

Thomas indicates the continuity of these specified precepts with the
first precept by re-iterating that these precepts aim for the good. But
"since...good has the nature of an end," we must specify the agent in
question, for particular natures act for specific, proper ends. Accordingly,
with regard to human action, it is necessary that we first discover the end
to which man as a species is directed.[35] This end is discovered, as it is
with all species, by observing the natural inclinations that manifest the
eternal law's providential directing of every nature. It is for this reason
that the ends of these inclinations "are naturally apprehended by reason as
being good, and consequently as objects of pursuit." Speculative reason
first grasps the truth of a nature; in understanding a nature, we come to
know which natural inclinations perfect that nature; this is the good at
which actions ought to aim. So, Thomas concludes, "according to the
order of natural inclinations, is the order of the precepts of the natural
law."

Thomas then specifies the sorts of inclinations man has. These inclinations are those inclinations that man has according to the transcendental property *being*, the genus *animal*, and the specific difference *rational*.[36] Man's inclinations to perfection are determined by his mode of participation in existence, not merely according to rationality but according
to the total specification of being in terms of human nature. First, human
beings, like all beings, will defend the first perfection of existence itself
and preserve themselves in being.[37] Second, man has inclinations accord-

[35] This direction is initially accomplished by means of the divine ideas' specification of
being, for the divine ideas distinguish natures according to their end (*De Veritate* 3.1.c.);
this is implicit in the idea of a providential creation, since every agent acts for an end (see
SCG III.97).

[36] This three-fold order of goods reflects the fundamental acts to be, to live, to understand, because these are the perfections that man is supposed to will for himself as an existent, sensate, rational being; see *ST* I-II.10.1.c., and I-II.10.2.ad 3.

[37] Cf. *De Veritate* 21.2.c.: "For whatever does not yet participate in the act of being
tends toward it by a certain natural appetite. In this way matter tends to form, according
to the Philosopher. But everything which already has being naturally loves its being and
with all its strength preserves it."

ing to his animality. These would be all the inclinations that stem from a sensitive nature (such as eating, sleeping, etc.) including, but not limited to, the examples of procreation and offspring-rearing mentioned.[38] Third, there are inclinations according to reason, which grasps universals and higher-level concepts, goods such as the common good of society and the ultimate end of man, the love of God.[39] Thomas concludes that "all these precepts of the law of nature have the character of one natural law, inasmuch as they flow from one first precept."[40] That is, because these precepts are founded wholly on the convertibility of the determinate mode of existence and its naturally dynamic perfective activity, they are both self-evident and universally binding.

The Derived Secondary and Tertiary Precepts of the Natural Law. As a short epilogue, I want to briefly indicate how those self-evident precepts relate to the derived, non-self-evident precepts of the natural law. The self-evident precepts of the natural law are self-evident inasmuch as both are founded on the convertibility of being and goodness, either the transcendental being and indeterminate good or the specific mode of existence and the perfection in terms of its proper operations. But these precepts are still too general to be of real guidance in concrete situations, for they pertain only to the most general aspects of life. (For example, *rear offspring, foster knowledge*, and *do not offend others* all lack the specificity required for truly helpful norms since they do not specify how to act.) Thomas argues, therefore, that there are more specific precepts which are derivations or determinations from the general precepts. These derived precepts, as more particular, are more contingent and so less evident.[41] It is primarily about these precepts that moral disagreements arise. As Thomas says: "The practical reason…is busied with contingent matters, about which human actions are concerned: and consequently,

---

[38] Note that the examples he mentions are those characteristics made necessary by the fact that animals as individuals do not enjoy an immortality, but gain immortality only through the reproduction of the species. Their "obligation," therefore, is primarily to the species and not to any personal immortality; see *De Veritate* 5.3.c.

[39] In *ST* I-II.100.11.c., Thomas identifies the two great commandments, love God and love your neighbor, as being self-evident; these are, in fact, the same precepts he specifies here.

[40] *ST* I-II.94.2.ad 1.

[41] *ST* I-II. 94.4 and 6.

although there is necessity in the general principles, the more we descend to matters of detail, the more frequently we encounter defects."[42]

These contingent secondary precepts are distinguished from the primary precepts because they apply the general precept to a determinate instance. It is this application that obscures the evidence of the precept. The example Thomas uses is that it is universally known that man should act according to reason (which is self-evident given knowledge of man's nature), but that while it reasonably follows that one ought to return deposited property, this is neither self-evident (for, as I would interpret it, it involves notions of property that are not inherent in the notion of man as a rational animal) nor is it universal, for exceptions are to be made, given the contingent circumstances, as the famous example of the sword and the madman makes clear.[43] It is because of this extension into specificity and contingency that secondary precepts can be blotted out or adapted in order to meet the circumstances.[44]

To illustrate this distinction more clearly, it is to be noted that Thomas most often identifies these secondary precepts, which are immediate conclusions from the self-evident precepts, with the precepts of the Decalogue.[45] The general, self-evident precepts are not part of the Decalogue because, as self-evident, there is no need to promulgate them.[46] So, for example, *love God* and *love your neighbor* are self-evident

---

[42] *ST* I-II.94.4.c.[43] See *ST* I-II.94.4.c.

[43] See *ST* I-II.94.4.c.

[44] *ST* I-II.94.6.c. Cf. the conclusion to I-II.94.4.c.: "Consequently, we must say that the natural law, as to general principles, is the same for all, both as to rectitude and as to knowledge. But as to certain matters of detail, which are conclusions, as it were, of those general principles, it is the same for all in the majority of cases, both as to rectitude and as to knowledge; and yet in some few cases it may fail, both as to rectitude, by reason of certain obstacles...and as to knowledge, since in some the reason is perverted by passion, or evil habit, or an evil disposition; thus, formerly, theft, although it is expressly contrary to the natural law, was not considered wrong among the Germans."

[45] *ST* I-II.100.11.c.

[46] See *ST* I-II.100.3.c.: "Consequently two kinds of precepts are not reckoned among the precepts of the Decalogue: viz., first general principles, for they need no further promulgation after being once imprinted on the natural reason to which they are self-evident; as, for instance, that one should do evil to no man, and other similar principles:—and, again those which the careful reflection of wise men shows to be in accord with reason; since the people receive these principles from God, through being taught by wise men."

in themselves once one understands human nature's natural ends and its intrinsic relations to *God* and *society*. But this does not yet indicate what specific actions to pursue or avoid. Thus, those precepts contained in the Decalogue which specify concrete actions must be something other than self-evident. Now, most recognize that these are not terribly detailed precepts; nevertheless, they are detailed enough so as to prohibit particular kinds of actions. As a result, there is required an acuity to understand when that precept should be applied to a particular circumstance. (For instance, not all acts of dishonest speaking are truly prohibited by the seventh commandment.) Moreover, as is manifest from everyday experience, these precepts can be blotted out from the heart of man by passion or miseducation,[47] and so are in need of being promulgated in the Decalogue as a gracious assistance to man.

This brings us to the third level of natural law: the determination or application of precepts in light of specific circumstances. It is here that man is most likely to fail, since this is so far removed from the general principles of being and is a very concrete determination by the practical intellect.[48] Indeed, it is because of this contingency that prudence becomes essential for the moral life of man as a connatural, or intrinsic, principle of judgment that works together with the extrinsic natural law. This contingency also explains why there is moral diversity despite the objective intelligibility of the self-evident precepts. Natural law can lead man infallibly to the good, but the vicissitudes of extending those precepts from their generalized admonitions about human nature to a specific situation opens ample opportunity for error even for reasonable persons. Thomas uses this point in his refutation of the argument against natural law based on the fact of moral diversity: while detailed applications of the natural law allow for diversity, the more universal principles are self-evident and can surehandedly guide man regardless of circumstantial differences.[49]

The natural law is man's rational participation in the eternal law. The eternal law is that which directs all being to their perfection. The natural

[47] See *ST* I-II. 94.4.c.

[48] *De Veritate* 16.2.ad 1. (Cf. *De Veritate* 17.1.ad 1.)

[49] See *Commentary on Aristotle's "Nicomachean Ethics"* V.12.1025-1029.

law emerges from practical reason's grasping the nature of action in terms of the natural dynamism of being toward perfection. Thus, in understanding human nature's end, practical reason establishes precepts which acts as a rule for the good of human nature. The first precept is merely a recognition of the fact all being tends to perfection is its natural activity. From this, in understanding human nature as a delimited mode of being, practical reason then prescribes precepts which point out the specific goods for mankind. The foundation for all this is the convertibility of being, truth, and goodness, a convertibility which ultimately functions as the foundation for morality in the natural law.

WHY DOUBLE EFFECT AND PROPORTIONALITY ARE NOT MORAL PRINCIPLES FOR ST. THOMAS

Peter A. Redpath

When many contemporary ethicists, including "Thomists," talk about St. Thomas Aquinas's moral teaching, they often refer to this teaching as a natural law moral philosophy. Within this context, especially when discussing "just war" theory, they also often refer to what they call the moral principles of "double effect" and "proportionality." They talk in these ways despite the fact that (1) St. Thomas was principally a Roman Catholic theologian, not a philosopher; (2) his moral teaching devotes little attention to a discussion of natural law, and, when he does discuss this issue, he does so in a handful of pages (about seven to ten in a standard contemporary paperback) and, partly, for the purpose of showing its inadequacy as a moral guide; and (3), strictly speaking, considered in and of themselves, for Aquinas, "double effect" and "proportionality" are not moral principles.

The above observations might startle many contemporary readers, including some Thomists. So, too, might what St. Thomas says in his introduction to his consideration of moral activity in the *Prima secundae* (First Part of the Second Part) of his *Summa theologiae*: "Next it is necessary to consider the exterior principles of action. The devil, about whose temptation we spoke in the prior section, is the exterior principle inclining us toward evil. And God, who teaches us through law and helps us through grace, is the exterior principle moving us toward good." The Latin text reads:

> Consequenter considerandum est de principiis exterioribus actuum. Principuum autem exterius ad malum inclinans est diabolus, de cuius tentatione in Primo dictum est. Principium autem exterius movens ad bonum est Deus, qui et nos instruit per legem et iuvat per gratiam.[1]

Elsewhere, I have defended in detail my above claims that, strictly speaking, St. Thomas is a Christian theologian, not a philosopher, and a

---

[1] St. Thomas Aquinas, *Summa theologiae*, ed. Piana (Ottawa: Collège Dominicain d'Ottawa, 1941), I-II, proem, q. 90.

Christian ethicist, not a natural law philosopher.[2] For this reason, I will not give a detailed defense of these claims in this article. Here, I will simply mention that, in making these assertions, I do not deny that St. Thomas uses philosophy in his theologizing or natural law in his Christian moralizing. I deny that, according to St. Thomas's reasoning principles, philosophy formally distinguishes his thought and that natural law formally distinguishes his moral thought. In a similar fashion, in this paper, while I admit that, consideration of proportionality and of a moral act that involves two effects plays some role in parts of St. Thomas's moral teaching, considered in and of themselves, strictly speaking, proportionality and two effects of a moral action do not play the role of moral principles in his moral thought.

Prior to discussing the exterior principles of moral activity, St. Thomas considers 89 questions examining principles related to the human subject, the faculties of human, or moral, activity, the intrinsic, or proximate, principles of moral activity: reason, appetition, and deliberate choice. He refers to these, not to natural law, as intrinsic moral principles. He does so precisely because these faculties are the proximate, *per se*, intrinsic, and chief, real, not logical, principles and causes of moral activity, a multitude of free activity proximately subjectified in and caused by living human agents.

In discussing St. Thomas's moral teaching, we need to recall that, for St. Thomas, philosophy is a *habitus* [a habit], not a logical system or body of knowledge. Like Aristotle before him, strictly speaking, Aquinas considered philosophy to be a human operation, the act of a human habit or

---

[2] See Peter A. Redpath, "Classifying the Moral Teaching of St. Thomas," *The Medieval Tradition of Natural Law*, ed. Harold J. Johnson (Kalamazoo, Mich.: Medieval Institute Publications, Studies in Medieval Culture XXII, 1987), pp. 137–148; "Maritain's Friendship with Aquinas," *Understanding Maritain: Philosopher and Friend*, ed. Deal W. Hudson and Matthew J. Mancini (Atlanta: Mercer University Press, 1987), pp. 91–113; "Philosophizing within Faith," *Faith and the Life of the Intellect*, ed. Curtis L. Hancock and Brendan Sweetman (Washington, D. C.: The Catholic University of America Press, 2003), pp. 93–123.

habitus. He did not primarily think of philosophy as a system or body of knowledge.[3]

For this reason, among others, he tells us that philosophy studies a real, not a logical, subject or genus, a proximate subject, or generic substance. While this subject resembles a logical genus because we include it in the definition of beings that participate in it (its intrinsic, or *per se*, accidents), strictly speaking, this subject genus of philosophical study is a substance considered as the real, or concrete, cause, of real, or concrete, effects: the proper subject of intrinsic, necessary operations, or *per se* accidents. Hence, he states:

> This sense of genus is not the one that signifies the essence of a species, as animal is the genus of man, but the one that is the proper subject in the species of different accidents. For surface is the subject of all plane figures. And it bears some likeness to a genus, because the proper subject is given in the definition of an accident just as a genus is given in the definition of its species. Hence the proper subject of an accident is predicated like a genus [4]

Surface is the immediate, proximate, subject, the "common matter," of all colors and plane figures. As such, it is the referential source of intelligibility, the necessary identity condition for the existence of, all surface bodies. All such figures and colors exist in dimensive substance. They get their identity conditions for being figured and colored bodies, by being proximately subjectified, and quantitatively and qualitatively unified, in a surface.

Aristotle maintains that a genus is a kind of whole, one that, for philosophy, or science, primarily refers to the immediate, proximate, first, or

---

[3] Armand A. Maurer, "The Unity of a Science: St. Thomas and the Nomina-lists," *St. Thomas Aquinas, 1274–1974, Commemorative Studies*, ed.-in-chief, Armand A. Maurer (Toronto: Pontifical Institute of Mediaeval Studies, 1974), vol. 2, pp. 269–291. See, also, Peter A. Redpath, "Philosophy's Non-Systematic Nature," *A Thomistic Tapestry: Essays in Memory of Étienne Gilson* (Amsterdam and New York: Editions Rodopi, B. V., 2002), pp. 29–36.

[4] St. Thomas Aquinas, *Commentary on the Metaphysics of Aristotle*, trans. John P. Rowan (Chicago: Henry Regnery Company, 1961), Bk. 5, l. 22, n. 1121.

proper subject of different *per se* accidents, or unities, within the genus.[5]
He further maintains that we cannot reduce one proximate subject to
another. Generically diverse beings are those "whose proximate substra-
tum is different, and which are not analyzed the one into the other nor
both into the same thing (e. g., form and matter are different in genus)."[6]

Thomas explains Aristotle's meaning by referring the idea of proximate subject to subjectifying, or common, matters. He says: "[A] solid is
in a sense reducible to surfaces, and therefore solid figures and plane figures do not belong to diverse genera, . . . but celestial bodies and lower
bodies are diverse in genus inasmuch as they do not have a common matter."[7] He adds, "In another sense those things are said to be diverse in
genus which are predicated 'according to a different figure of the catego-
ry of being,' i.e., of the predication of being."[8] He immediately notes,
however, that the natural scientist and metaphysician consider a genus as
the first subject of accidents, not as what is said of different categories of
being, which is the way a logician considers generic diversity:

> Now it is clear, from what has been said, that some things are
> contained under one category and are in one genus in this sec-
> ond sense, although they are diverse in genus in the first sense.
> Examples of these are the celestial bodies, and colors and fla-
> vors. The first way in which things are diverse in genus is con-
> sidered rather by the natural scientist and also by the philoso-
> pher [that is, the metaphysician], because it is more real. But
> the second way in which things are diverse in a genus is con-
> sidered by the logician, because it is conceptual.[9]

According to St. Thomas, we derive this notion of a genus from the
"common matter" that two beings share. And he maintains that the job of
philosophers is to reflect *chiefly* upon this proximate, first, subject (a concrete, universal cause) and upon its intrinsic and necessary, or *per se*,

[5] Aristotle, *Metaphysics*, trans. W. D. Ross, in *The Basic Works of Aristotle*, ed.
Richard Mc Keon (New York: Random House, 1941, 21st printing, 1968), Bk. 5, 24,
1023a26–32, and 26, 1024a29–1024b4.

[6] Aristotle, *Metaphysics*, Bk. 5, 28, 1024b10–13.

[7] Aquinas, *Commentary on the Metaphysics of Aristotle*, Bk. 5, l. 22, n. 1125.

[8] *Ibid.*, n. 1126.

[9] *Ibid.*, n. 1127. Bracketed material is my addition.

accidents (its concrete effects), a hierarchical order of species, contrary opposites, that flow from it.

At the start of Aristotle's *Metaphysics*, St. Thomas explains that the proximate subject, or generic substance, about which the geometrician wonders is the surface body, the body that is the immediate, chief, proximate, and principle subject, or cause, of all plane figures, its intrinsic and necessary, or *per se*, accidents. By this he means that the quantified body is the formal object, the "common matter," that geometricians study, in contrast to the qualified body (the formal object that physicists study) and the substantial and non-substantial body (the formal object that metaphysicians study). These different modes of bodily being, thought about as formal objects of consideration, are essentially connected to Aristotle's threefold division of the speculative sciences into physics, mathematics, and metaphysics.

Plane figures comprise a multitude of beings, of hierarchically ordered opposites, or species (a many) potentially subjectified in a surface body, their "common matter." They essentially flow from this proximate body as from a concrete principle or universal cause (a one). For this reason, Aristotle maintained that science is always a study of the universal [the concrete, not logical, universal]. Since this is the body that proximately causes these necessary and intrinsic accidents, it is their *per se*, or proper, subject, and proximate cause, or principle, and they are its *per se*, or proper, accidents. Much in the same way, Socrates the musician, not Socrates the philosopher, or Socrates the human being, is the proper and *per se* principle, cause, and subject of flute playing, which is his proper or *per se* accident. Or, as Socrates tells Thrasymachos in Book 1 of Plato's *Republic*, strictly speaking, the physician, not the money-maker, is a healer of the sick.[10] The fact that a physician might also be a money-maker is incidental to the fact that the person doing the healing is a healer. This is because the physician heals through the healing habit, not through the money-making habit.

The surface body is the subject, matter, or genus, or generic substance upon which the geometrician primarily reflects, for the purpose of considering how the principles of this subject give rise to, or concretely

[10] Plato, *Republic*, Bk. 1, 340C–342E, 343A–347E.

cause, its different species, or *per se* accidents or concrete effects.[11] Analogously, we may say that the medical doctor studies the relatively healthy human body, the human body as the subject of extreme differences, contrary opposites, of different species of human health and disease because the proximate subject or principle of health and disease is the living, sentient, human body, not the substantial body, or surface body. We may say that the subject the ethicist studies is the moral body, that is, the free human subject, which is the proximate principle of the moral species of actions that proceed from human choice, the contrary opposites consisting of moral virtue and vice. We may say that the economist studies the economic body, the free social human body engaged in exchanges by which we become instrumentally rich or poor. Or that the politician studies the political body, or body politic: the free social human body naturally engaged in the pursuit of healthy, and avoidance of unhealthy, social life, or more simply pursuing peace and avoiding war.

The import for us of St. Thomas's teaching about the nature of a subject of a science is that Thomas considered ethics to be a practical science that studies a multitude, but not an infinite number, of beings in light of proximate moral principles. For this reason, his discussion of the relation of two effects to moral choice and moral activity occurs within the context of divisions of vices opposed to the divisions of the moral virtue of justice, introduced in Question 63 of the *Secunda secundae* (Second Part of the Second Part) of the *Summa theologiae*.

Prior to this dicussion, St. Thomas has divided justice into two general parts: (1) distributive, or administrative; and (2) commutative, or justice related to transactions between individuals. After doing this, because philosophy, or science, studies opposites within a genus, St. Thomas says he has to consider the two vices, or sins, opposed to the divisions, or parts, of justice: (1) personal favoritism (*acceptio personarum*) as the vice opposed to distributive justice and (2) voluntary and involuntary injuries in word or deed involving personal transactions between people, as vices opposed to the virtue of commutative justice. The Latin text introducing Question 63 starts:

---

[11] Aquinas, *Commentary on the Metaphysics of Aristotle*, Bk. 5, l. 22, n. 1121, 1125–1127; Aristotle, *Metaphysics*, Bk. 5, 28, 1024b10–13.

> Deinde considerandum est de vitiis oppositis praedictis iustiti-
> ae partibus. Et primo, de acceptione personarum, quae opponi-
> tur iustitiae distributivae; secundo, de peccatis quae opponun-
> tur iustitiae commutativae.

Question 63 considers the injustice of personal favoritism that opposes the virtue of distributive justice. Question 64 starts the examination of
a multitude of vices opposed to the virtue of commutative justice.

St. Thomas considers these vices according to the sorts of transactions in which injury can happen (voluntary or involuntary), the means
through which an injury is executed (word or deed), and the subject upon
which an injury is inflicted (a person, someone related to a person, or a
person's property). His proem to the Question 64 begins:

> Postea considerandum est de vitiis oppositis commutativae
> iustitiae. Et primo considerandum est de peccatis quae com-
> mittuntur circa involuntarias commutationes; secundo, de pec-
> catis quae committuntur circa commutationes voluntarias.
> Committuntur autem peccata circa involuntarias commuta-
> tiones per hoc quod aliquod nocumentum proximo infertur
> contra eius voluntatem, quod quidem potest fieri dupliciter,
> scilicet facto et verbo. Facto quidem cum proximus laeditur vel
> in persona propria, vel in persona coniuncta, vel in propriis
> rebus.

St. Thomas starts his examination of commutative injustices in
Question 64 by considering homicide, the greatest injury we can inflict
upon our neighbor. He divides this Question into eight articles. The first
seven consider the legitimacy of: (1) killing brute animals and plants; (2)
killing sinners; (3) private or public individuals committing homicide; (4)
clerics committing homicide; (5) suicide; (6) killing a just man; (7)
killing in self-defense. Article 8 considers whether accidental killing is
mortally sinful.

St. Thomas's discusses the moral status of an action having two
effects in Question 64, Article 7, related to the issue of the moral legitimacy of self-defense. In resolving the problem under consideration,
Thomas explains that nothing prohibits one action from having two
effects, one that an agent intends and another that is outside an agent's
intention. Since moral acts are acts we directly cause, freely caused prac-

tical acts, acts necessarily caused by and, therefore, related to our personal powers of free causation, Thomas tells us that we specify human acts as moral from what an agent intends (a final cause), not from what is extraneous to personal intention (for example, a secondary, or incidental, act). Strictly speaking, unintended acts are incidental to moral acts considered as such, or moral acts considered *per se*, because they bear an accidental, not a necessary, or essential, relation to the acts under consideration. Personal intention, the human good intended, however, is a final cause of practical human action. It essentially issues from ourselves as free agents. Hence, it bears an essential relation to the choice under consideration and directly and essentially relates to the action as a formal moral principle or object.

In the case of the practical sciences, these formal principles are habits, or qualities, inhering in our intellectual faculty ordered toward human choice. Such being the case, in some way, necessity, must activate them. Necessity is the mark of science. Science is thinking about what must be. Hence, even if practical thinking is essentially ordered to thinking about contingent events, what makes our practical way of thinking *scientific* is that we possess our concrete, practical habit of thinking in relation to consideration of necessary, not contingent or incidental, relations to a proximate object, or goal, considered as related *per se* to a proximate subject, or agent, considered *per se*.

We derive our practical *per se*, or formal, object, in short, according to differences between actions we can practically consider. We derive these differences partly from a consideration of (1) the magnitude of the difficulty we face (the subject under consideration) in practical action, and (2) the way that subject relates to our human powers and habits: what we intend and are capable of choosing in the face of this subject; and the moral virtue that perfects our choice, the means we may reasonably choose to achieve our end.

St. Thomas tells us that we take the methods of the sciences "from the powers of the soul" because science is an acquired mental power, a habit, and these powers, or habits, operate in different ways. He says that we determine how our powers, or habits, operate by relating them to their *per se* objects, objects that necessarily and proximately cause or activate them (like color activates the eyes and sound the ears, unjust attack activates our habit of just defense, or a diseased body activates our medical habit). Hence, we take the methods of moral science partly from the different *per se* objects, or identity conditions, that determine a proximate subject (for example, a just defender) necessarily to react, in one way, not another, in this way (for example, justly), not that (for example, unjustly).[12]

Because moral science is practical, it must involve our intellects in wondering about how to generate effects from our personal powers in the hope of calling up *per se* principles of practical actions, appropriate moral virtues as proximate causes of our action here and now. Hence, from the side of the power of the intellect, will, and human emotions, from the part of the intentional agent, we partly derive a *per se* object, or aim, that essentially activates our intellects as acting practically, some good that we seek as a human good (for example, self-preservation).

Our thinking is practical partly because we have some sort of faculty or power capable of generating practical acts in relation to real human goods. Our scientific habits are practical precisely because they conform to the ontological exigencies of the human intellect, will, and emotions aiming at choosing a real human good, because these exigencies involve us in thinking about necessities, about means necessarily related to the ends we, as human beings, intend.

Scientifically, we proceed in this way because we derive scientific principles partly from the natural constitution of our faculties and partly from the way things exist according to mind-independent relations. Scientifically, we think and choose the way we can (according to the way our powers operate in relation to different *per se* objects, like the power of Socrates the flute-player operates in relation to the-musical-instrument-the-flute), not the way we wish. The being of things and the way this essentially relates to our natural faculties determine the methods (that is, the habits as necessarily ordered toward their formal objects) by which we can think about, and choose objects, at all or scientifically. Hence, the being of things and the natural constitution of our knowing powers provide the unity and necessity that ground all knowledge and science.

12 Armand A. Maurer (ed.), *Commentary on the de Trinitate of Boethius, Questions V and VI. St. Thomas Aquinas: The Division and Methods of the Sciences* (Toronto: Pontifical Institute of Mediaeval Studies, 1963), q. 6, a. 1, reply to 4.

Since, for Aquinas, our practical intellect is a faculty directly ordered to concrete action, it must consider the individual, contingent circumstances under which we operate, a plurality of possible, not impossible, choices. These circumstances essentially participate in activating our moral responses (just as the existence of unhealthy bodies generates the intellect's doctoring inclination or habit). A necessary identity condition of the *per se* object of practical science is that it be a proximate subject materially, or concretely, considered. In short, what makes our thinking practical is that we think about a concretely considered proximate subject simply as such, like the person engaged in self-defense must think about a person considered as an attacker, not as simply as another human being, and of the right moral means (the appropriate moral virtue or virtues) that essentially relate to fending off such an attacker. Even though we are acting in time and under contingent circumstances, the attacker-as-attacker bears an essential relation to us as defenders and the defensive means we choose to react to an attacker bear a necessary relation of defensive reactions to an attack.

In the case under consideration, St. Thomas maintains that an act of self-defense can have a twofold effect: (1) the essentially-intended preservation of the defensive agent's life, and (2) the incidental killing of an attacker. Because all physical beings have a natural desire for self-preservation, Thomas adds that the act of self-defense must be morally legitimate. When analogously transposed the human level, the natural good of self-preservation acts as a moral principle, a final cause, giving human beings the moral right, or legitimacy, to engage in self-defense.

St. Thomas's conclusion in this situation is simply an instance of him analogously transposing the metaphysical principle of eternal law toward operation on the human level. The fact that eternal law commands all beings to preserve themselves according to their natures, or according to the order of their natural inclinations, is a metaphysical principle. On the moral level, this translates into the necessity for human beings to seek to preserve ourselves the way human beings are naturally inclined to do: through use of our reason and virtue according to the natural order of subordination of powers and priority of ends in and through which we are naturally inclined to operate. In this instance, eternal law is a remote, not a proximate, cause of our moral action. Strictly speaking, the operative moral principle is justice, not eternal, or natural, law.

Given this understanding, St. Thomas cautions us that, while acting out of a good intention gives us a legitimate moral claim to self-defense, specification of a moral act as completely good depends upon our acting in moderation. Hence, he says that, if our action is not proportionate to our end, it becomes morally illegitimate.

The reason for this is not that proportionality as such is a moral principle. The operative moral principle in question is the moral virtue of justice, not the quantitative relation of proportionality. Considered as such, quantitative relations have no moral status. The moral virtue of justice demands that we moderate our actions toward our neighbors so that we answer unjust violence with a just amount of defensive action. All virtues are moral qualities whose being consists in exercise of moderation in human choice. Proportionality is only a moral principle in a relational sense inasmuch as it comprises a property of moral virtue. And it is an attribute of moral virtue because moral virtues are qualities and because, for St. Thomas, qualities are essentially intensive quantities.

Qualities are existential conditions that make possible transmission of action. Things act through their qualities [like musical sound acts through speakers of a specific quality or just actions act through the virtue of justice]. Hence, qualities are natural intrinsic limits, or limits of conductive capacity, within a thing's natural potency for action. For this reason, the better a thing's quality, the better its action. Hence, no quality, or totally bad quality, no action.

St. Thomas explains his teaching about qualities as intensive quantities in a distinction he makes, following Aristotle, between two general divisions of quantity. He says : "Quantity is twofold. One is called bulk (*molis*) quantity or dimensive (*dimensiva*) quantity, which is the only kind of quantity in bodily things. . . . The other is virtual (*virtutis*) quantity, which occurs according to the perfection of some nature or form." He adds that this sort of quantity is also called "spiritual greatness just as heat is called great because of its intensity and perfection."[13] He elaborates his point thus:

---

[13] St. Thomas Aquinas, *Summa theologiae*, I, 42, 2, ad 1. See also, I-II, 52, 1, respondeo. For a more extensive treatment of the notion of virtual quantity in Aristotle and Aquinas, see C. B. Crowley, *Aristotelian-Thomistic Philosophy of Measure and the International System of Units (SI)*, ed. Peter A. Redpath (Lanham, Md.: University Press of America, 1996), pp. 25–47, 249–260.

> [E]ach thing is perfect when no part of the natural magnitude
> which belongs to it according to the form of its proper ability
> is missing. Moreover, just as each natural being has a definite
> measure of natural magnitude in continuous quantity, as is stat-
> ed in Book II of *The Soul*, so too each thing has a definite
> amount of its own natural ability. For example, a horse has by
> nature a definite dimensive quantity, within certain limits; for
> there is both a maximum quantity and minimum quantity
> beyond which no horse can go in size. And in a similar way the
> quantity of active power in a horse which is not in fact sur-
> passed in any horse; and similarly there is some minimum
> which never fails to be attained.[14]

In other words, qualities, like, color, or justice, wisdom, science,
or courage are kinds of intrinsic magnitudinal limits, intensities. Their
mode of being consists in their being intrinsic limits of the greater or less
perfection, completeness, of a thing's action or motion. St. Thomas says
that we get this notion of intensive quantity, or quality, analogously from
the way we predicate perfection, or completeness, of dimensive quantity.
We then transfer this notion to qualities.

He adds that qualities are of basically two sorts: (1) essential differences and (2) differences, or alterations, of bodies capable of motion, like
hot and cold, heavy and light, black and white. This second sense refers
to the way we generally use the term "quality" "of virtue and vice, and,
in general, of evil and good," and, therefore, of intensive quantity
(because it involves completeness of perfection of form).[15] Aristotle considers quality in this sense to be an accident related to motion or action,
an intensive quantitative modification of something moved or acted upon
inasmuch as it is moved or acted upon, an intrinsic limit of receptive
capacity or completeness in action. Consequently, regarding virtue and
vice, Aristotle says:

> Virtue and vice fall among these modifications; for they indi-
> cate differentiae of the movement or activity, according to
> which the things in motion act or are acted upon well or badly;

---

[14] Aquinas, *Commentary on the Metaphysics of Aristotle*, vol. 1, Bk. 5, L. 18, n. 1037.
[15] *Ibid.*, Bk. 5, L. 16, nn. 987–999.

for that which can be moved or act in one way is good and that
which can do so in another, the contrary way, is vicious. Good
and evil indicate quality especially in living things, and among
these especially in those which have purpose.16

St. Thomas comments upon Aristotle's reference to virtues and vices
enabling us to move "well" or "badly" that these terms *chiefly* relate to
living things and "especially" to those possessed of "choice." Thomas
explains that he makes this comment because living things particularly
act for an end and "rational beings, in whom alone choice exists know
both the end and the proportion of the means to the end."17

Part of St. Thomas's point in the above block quote is that quality
modifies a motion or action by placing an action within bounds. In this
way, it gives the action order and proportion, properties that arise from
quantity as such. In so doing, quality gives an motion intelligibility, especially in connection to acting for an end. Quality does this because, as a
species of quantity, quality imparts these essentially quantitative properties of order and limits to that in which it inheres.18

St. Thomas maintains that we are incapable of directly comparing
any two qualities. He says that quality as quality only directly relates to
the subject in which exists. Its being is a referential being to its subject.
We can only relate one quality to another by referring the one to the other
(1) as an active or passive potency of the other, as being a principle or
source of acting or being acted upon (like heating and being heated) or (2)
through reference to quantity or something related quantity, as, for example, when we say that one thing is hotter than another because its quality
of heat is more intense.19

Taken in conjunction with Aristotle's teaching on contraries, this
inability directly to compare two qualities throws light on how Aristotle
and St. Thomas understand the nature of virtue as a mean and a measure
of proportion in moral action. For Aristotle contrariety is one of the four

16 Aristotle, *Metaphysics*, Bk. 5, ch. 14, 1020b18–25.

17 Aquinas, *Commentary on the Metaphysics of Aristotle*, vol. 1, Bk. 5, L. 16, n. 998.

18 Maurer (ed.), *Commentary on the de Trinitate of Boethius, Questions V and VI. St. Thomas Aquinas: The Division and Methods of the Sciences* (Toronto: Pontifical Institute of Mediaeval Studies, 1963), q. 5, a. 3, reply to 3.

19 Aquinas, *Commentary on the Metaphysics of Aristotle*, Bk. 10, l. 2, n. 1008.

kinds of opposition: (1) contradiction, (2) contrariety, (3) privation, and (4) relation.[20] Contraries are forms, extreme differences, or specific extremes or limits, within the same genus between which a mean, middle, or intermediary can exist. This mean or middle relates to both extremes as a one, intermediate, or midpoint between possession and privation. It is neither extreme, relates to both, and is opposed to both by an opposition of privative negation, not of contrariety, just as, for example, the midpoint between the extremely hot and extremely cold is nor hot or cold but can become both, or a morally neutral person is not morally good or bad but can become both.[21]

Aristotle tells us that some changes from one contrary to another involve a necessary passage through a midpoint. This midpoint stands in a condition of equality and private negation in relation to both extremes, just as passage from the great to the small and the fast to the slow must pass through what is equidistant from, and deprived of, both. Hence, because the equal stands as a mean or midpoint between extremes of possession and deprivation of a form within a genus, we can use it as a measure for knowing both extremes.[22]

In relationship to the equal, which is a one, two opposites exist, comprising the unequal (in this case, excess and defect of some form). Analogously speaking, these inequalities are multiplicities or pluralities. This means that we can measure qualitative differences, or difference of intensity in possession of a quality, by comparing excessive and deprived possession to possession of equal, or neutral, intensity. We can compare one quality to another by relating both the qualities we wish to compare to a third quality that stands midway between them in intensity, much like we can compare the heaviness of two different bodies through use of a balance scale that compares their weight relative to a state of equilibrium.

---

[20] Aristotle, *Metaphysics*, Bk. 10, 4, 1055a33–1055b3.

[21] *Ibid.*, 1056a10–30.

[22] Aquinas, *Commentary on the Metaphysics of Aristotle*, Bk. 10, l. 7, nn. 2059-2074. For extensive analysis of the way contemporary physical scientists use the equal as a measure, see Crowley, *Aristotelian-Thomistic Philosophy of Measure and the International System of Units (SI)*.

This qualitative state becomes the measure of the other two and the principle by which we know them.[23]

We can now easily see how Aristotle and St. Thomas apply this teaching about contrariety and the comparison of qualities to virtue and ethics. Like all sciences, ethics studies a genus of being grounded in a specific kind of matter, a "common matter": moral matter. Active and passive potencies qualify this moral matter. Specifically, moral matter is a genus (a free human agent) subject to opposing habits of human choice. Ethics studies this moral body, the free human agent, as a principle of many possible opposing acts open to human choice, to try to comprehend the qualitative potentialities and properties that constitute human choice, to comprehend the powers of the soul as motive principles that can act well or badly. This science seeks to understand to comprehend human choice as the principle and cause of the many free acts that we human beings perform and to enable morally virtuous people to act better as human beings and cause morally vicious people to be deprived of perfection in human action. To engage in this study moral philosophers must examine a multiplicity of human acts because we can only comprehend power and potentiality in relation to actuality.

According to Aristotle and St. Thomas, all science seeks to understand its subject matter in terms of its principles and causes. They also say that the first, or maximum, in any genus is the cause and measure of all that is in the genus. This means that every genus contains a species that has a form existing in its most complete state. This species is the locus of the form most glaringly present, present in its maximum of intensive quantity. Hence, all science seeks to find this species of its genus to help us use our understanding of its powers and properties as a means for knowing the powers and properties of its more deprived members.

In the case of moral science, the genus of moral agency, the maximum in the genus, the starting point of moral reasoning, lies in the habits of the prudent person and in reason's general certainty that a greatest intensive quantity of qualified act (a greatest human good, happiness) exists for beings that possess the human form. The prudent person is the rule or measure of all moral science. As the contrary opposite of the

[23] Crowley, *Aristotelian-Thomistic Philosophy of Measure and the International System of Units (SI)*, p. 28.

imprudent person, the prudent person is the maximum in the genus of moral choice. Hence, we have to use the behavior of the prudent person to comprehend goodness about human action. As the privative opposite of the extremes of imprudent moral excess and defect within the same genus, the prudent person is the intermediate, the equal, in the same genus, who acts like a balance scale to enable us to compare and contrast moral virtue and viciousness.[24] In this person we find (1) the quality of active human powers exercised with their maximum of intensive quantity, or completeness of form, human goodness, and (2) the balance, or equal state, between extremes of too much and too little intensive quantity of chosen action.[25]

For Aristotle and St. Thomas, in short, moral science starts from the evidently accepted principle, or preamble, that all human beings by nature have a greatest or maximum human desire: to live well and a multiplicity of contrary and opposing habits of actions that moral science studies to find the principles for living well, the maximum of which we find achieved in the actions and habits of the prudent person.

Aristotle tells us, "Virtue is a state of character concerned with choice, lying in a mean, i.e. the mean relative to us, this being determined by a rational principle, and by that principle by which the man of practical wisdom would determine it." As mean between two vices, virtue is an intermediate, equal, or right state, or state of intermediary intensive quantity, standing between, and opposed by an opposition of privative negation, not of contrariety, to two contrary vicious opposites of excess and defect of right measure in action and being acted upon.[26] As such, virtue is a standard of proportionality in moral action.

---

[24] Aristotle, *Nicomachean Ethics*, trans. W. D. Ross, in *The Basic Works of Aristotle*, Bk. 2, 5, 1106b36–1107a2, Bk. 3, 4, 1113a31–33. See, also, Joseph Owens, "The Grounds of Ethical Universality in Aristotle," *Aristotle: The Collected Papers of Joseph Owens*, ed. John R. Catan (Albany, NY: SUNY Press, 1981), pp. 148–164, and Richard P. Geraghty, *The Object of Moral Philosophy According to St. Thomas Aquinas* (Washington, D.C.: University Press of America, 1982), pp. 56–61.

[25] For an excellent exposition of St. Thomas's moral teaching as a practical and prudential science, see Richard Geraghty, "The Practical Nature of Moral Philosophy," *A Thomistic Tapestry*, pp. 13–28.

[26] Aristotle, *Nicomachean Ethics*, Bk. 2, 6, 1107a1–8.

For this reason, the courageous person is the intermediate between the reckless person and the timid. And a person who seeks to hit the mean between contrary vices must proceed toward the mean, the right measure, a specific intensive quantity of action that equals the best state of exercising our faculty of choice in the here and now.[27] Habituation of the good person determines the right answer in moral choice, the answer equal to the situation and an agent's natural and habituated powers, precisely because this person has experience of virtue, of the equal in matters open to inequality, or plurality, of action.[28]

This is not to say that moral science only studies the behavior of prudent people. St. Thomas tells us that every science chiefly studies one subject present, with different degrees of intensive quantity, in a multiplicity of different, opposite, and contrary beings. Secondarily and analogously it studies a multiplicity of other things that essentially relate in varying degrees to this one subject. For example, a dentist must study dental instruments and a lawyer must read law books. In the case of moral science, the one subject is human action as we find this extremely opposed in virtue and vice. But Aristotle thinks that the moral philosopher must also take into account and evaluate other things that essentially relate to development of moral virtue and vice, such as moral education and culture.[29]

In so doing, however, the ethician can never lose sight of the fact that (1) the chief object of moral science is a proper subject whose *per se* principles this science seeks to grasp, and (2) we can grasp no *per se* principle without reference to the notion of unity and intensive quantity and to our human faculties and habits to which this principle essentially relates.

In a similar fashion, without an understanding of St. Thomas's notion of intensive quantity and his teaching about the nature of science as a habit and the division and methods of the sciences, none of us can adequately grasp his moral teaching. Hence, the inclination of so many contemporary Thomists incorrectly to equate St. Thomas's moral teaching with a simple natural law philosophy, generally to misunderstand his

27 *Ibid.*, Bk. 2, 8, 1109a1–36.

28 *Ibid.*, Bk. 1, 2, 1095a1–12, Bk. 1, 8, 1099a13–24, Bk. 2, 6, 1106b36–1107a2.

29 Owens, "The Grounds of Ethical Universality in Aristotle," pp. 156–157.

teaching about moral science and moral principles, and mistakenly to attribute to him moral principles like "double effect" and "proportionality." We owe St. Thomas and our readers better treatment.

THOMAS AQUINAS ON THE NATURAL DESIRE
FOR A SUPERNATURAL END

Mark D. Gossiaux

The concept of natural desire plays an important role in Thomas Aquinas' ethical thought. In his well known discussion of ST I-II 94.2, Thomas derives several natural law precepts by appealing to man's natural inclinations. He observes that humans have a natural inclination to preserve their own lives, to rear offspring, to know the truth about God, and to live in society. The knowledge of God, however, is not merely *a* good for human beings; it is the *ultimate end* of human life, constituting man's *perfect good*. Human happiness is found only in the vision of God. This is an end, however, that human beings cannot achieve by their own efforts. With regard to its attainment, one may regard this end as supernatural. Thus one may speak of human beings as having a natural desire for a supernatural end.

A vast amount of secondary literature has accumulated concerning the coherence of Thomas' arguments on this issue. Much of it concerns the theological implications of his teaching.[1] In this paper I wish to focus purely on the philosophical status of his position. Did Thomas believe that philosophical reason can come to know that human happiness is only found in the vision of God? did he think that human beings have a natural desire for the beatific vision? or does he maintain instead that it is only by faith that human beings know of their ultimate end and desire to obtain it? There is a certain tension in his position: sometimes he affirms, at other times he denies the naturalness of man's desire for God.[2]

The present paper analyses Thomas' teaching on the natural desire for happiness, and attempts to show that his position is ultimately consistent. It is divided into three parts. Part I examines at those texts which purport to show that the desire for the vision of God is a natural one. Part

---

[1] See for example, Juan Alfaro, *Lo natural y lo sobrenatural: Estudio historico desede Santo Tomas hasta Cayetan (1274-1534)* (Burgos: Matriti, 1952); Henri de Lubac, *Surnaturel: études historiques* (Paris: Aubier, 1946); *The Mystery of the Supernatural*, tr. Rosemary Sheed (New York: Herder and Herder, 1967); and more recently, Denis J.M. Bradley, *Aquinas on the Twofold Human Good: Reason and Human Happiness in Aquinas's Moral Science* (Washington, DC.: Catholic University Press, 1997).

[2] The finest study of this topic remains that of Jorge Laporta, *La destinée de la nature humaine selon Thomas d'Aquin* (Paris: J. Vrin, 1965).

II looks at those texts which appear to deny the naturalness of this vision. Part III attempts to show that Thomas' position is consistent.

I

Thomas presents a rigorous analysis of the nature of human happiness in the third book of his *Summa Contra Gentiles* (1259-64).[3] His discussion there reveals the deep influence of Aristotle. After establishing that every agent acts for the sake of an end (c. 2), and hence for a good (c. 3), Thomas then shows (c. 17) that all things are ordered to a single ultimate end, namely, God. His reasoning is grounded on the claim that God is the highest good (*summum bonum*). Since what is greatest is any genus is a cause of all things in that genus, Thomas argues that God, as the highest good, must be the ultimate end, since he is the cause of the goodness of all other goods and of the finality of all other ends.[4]

Through their actions all creatures seek to acquire a likeness to the divine goodness. Each creature achieves this likeness in accordance with its nature; thus intellectual creatures do this by understanding God (*intelligere Deum*). In SCG III.25 Thomas brings forth a series of arguments to show that the ultimate end of intellectual substances consists in a knowledge of God. One argument is based on the nature of understanding. Thomas reasons that the proper activity of any thing is its end (since activity is its second perfection), and the goodness of a thing consists in the goodness of its operation. Thus the ultimate end of a thing consists in its most perfect activity. In the case of intellectual substances, understanding (*intelligere*) is their proper activity. However, since operations of this kind receive their specification from their objects, it is necessary that the degree of perfection of these activities should be in accordance with the degree of perfection of their objects. Thus the ultimate end of an intel-

---

[3] For the dating of Thomas' texts I shall follow J.-P. Torrell, *Saint Thomas Aquinas*, vol. 1: *The Person and his Work*, tran. R. Royal (Washington, DC.: Catholic University of America Press, 1996).

[4] SCG III, 17 (ed. Leonina Manualis, 241). See in particular: "*Quod est maximum in unoquoque genere, est causa omnium illorum quae sunt illius generis* [*Meta*. II.1, 993b22ff]; sicut ignis, qui est calidissimus, est causa caliditatis in aliis corporibus. Summum igitur bonum, quod est Deus, est causa bonitatis in omnibus bonis. Ergo et est causa cuiuslibet finis quod sit finis: cum quicquid est finis, sit huiusmodi inquantum est bonum...Deus igitur maxime est omnium rerum finis."

lectual substance consists in understanding the most perfect intelligible object, namely God.[5]

Thomas then takes note of an interesting objection. Granted that the ultimate end of an intellectual substance is to understand the most intelligible object, it does not follow that the most intelligible object of this or that intellectual substance is the most intelligible object absolutely (*simpliciter*). It might be the case that the higher the intellectual substance, the more perfect will be its intelligible object. Thus the highest intellectual substance would have for its ultimate end the knowledge of God, while a lower intellectual substance (a human soul for example) would be ordered to a lesser intelligible object. Thomas' response to this objection is clear and decisive:

> the end of any intellectual substance, even the lowest, is to understand God. For it was shown earlier that the ultimate end towards which all beings tend is God. Although the human intellect is lowest in the order of intellectual substances, still it is superior to all things lacking intellect. Therefore, since of a more noble substance there should not be a more ignoble end, the end of the human intellect also will be God himself.[6]

Granted that God is the ultimate end of all things, and that human beings are superior in perfection to nonhuman animals, it cannot be the case that the latter have God as their ultimate end while human beings do not.

---

[5] See SCG III, 25 (Leonina Manualis, 251): "Propria operatio cuiuslibet rei est finis eius: est enim secunda perfectio ipsius; unde quod ad propriam operationem bene se habet, dicitur virtuosum et bonum. Intelligere autem est propria operatio substantiae intellectualis. Ipsa igitur est finis eius. Quod igitur est perfectissimum in hac operatione, hoc est ultimus finis: et praecipue in operationibus quae non ordinantur ad aliqua operata, sicut est intelligere et sentire. Cum autem huiusmodi operationes ex obiectis speciem recipiant, per quae etiam cognoscuntur, oportet quod tanto sit perfectior aliqua istarum operationum, quanto eius obiectum est perfectius. Et sic intelligere perfectissimum intelligibile, quod Deus est, est perfectissimum in genere huius operationis quae est intelligere. Cognoscere igitur Deum intelligendo est ultimus finis cuiuslibet intellectualis substantiae."

[6] SCG III.25 (ed. Leonina Manualis, 252): "finis cuiuslibet substantiae intellectualis, etiam infimae, est intelligere Deum. Ostensum est enim supra quod omnium entium ultimus finis in quem tendunt, est Deus. Intellectus autem humanus, etsi sit infimus in ordine intellectualium substantiarum, est tamen superior omnibus intellectu carentibus. Cum ergo nobilioris substantiae non sit ignobilior finis, erit etiam intellectus humani finis ipse Deus."

Other arguments in this same chapter highlight the familiar Aristotelian claim that all human beings desire to know. One argument emphasizes the fact that knowledge is a grasp of causes. Thomas observes that all men naturally desire to know the causes of things; indeed, it was on account of their wonder about things which they could not explain that men first began to philosophize, and, upon discovering the cause of these things, their minds found rest. Now inquiry does not stop until the *first* cause is reached. Therefore, man naturally desires as his ultimate end to know the first cause. Since the first cause is God, Thomas concludes that the ultimate end for human beings is to know God.[7]

Another argument rests on the claim that only God satisfies that desire that is paradigmatically human:

> Man naturally desires to know the cause of any known effect. But the human intellect knows being universally. Therefore, it desires to know its cause, which is God alone, as was proven in the second book. However, there is no attainment of the ultimate end until man's natural desire is satisfied. Hence for human happiness, which is the ultimate end, no intelligible cognition suffices unless divine cognition is present, which terminates natural desire as its ultimate end. Therefore, the ultimate end of man is the knowledge of God.[8]

Man's happiness is located in that end that terminates his natural desire to know. However, the natural desire to know is satisfied only by the knowledge of the first cause of being, namely, God. Therefore, human happiness can be found only in the knowledge of God.

---

[7] See SCG III.25 (ed. Leonina Manualis, 253): "Naturaliter inest omnibus hominibus desiderium cognoscendi causas eorum quae videntur: unde propter admirationem eorum quae videbantur, quorum causae latebant, homines primo philosophari coeperunt, invenientes autem causam quiescebant. Nec sistit inquisitio quousque perveniatur ad primam causam.... Desiderat igitur homo naturaliter cognoscere primam causam quasi ultimum finem. Prima autem omnium causa Deus est. Est igitur ultimus finis hominis cognoscere Deum."

[8] Ibid. "Cuiuslibet effectus cogniti naturaliter homo scire causam desiderat. Intellectus autem humanus cognoscit ens universale. Desiderat igitur naturaliter cognoscere causam eius, quae solum Deus est, ut in Secundo probatum est. Non est autem aliquis assecutus finem ultimum quousque naturale desiderium quiescat. Non sufficit igitur ad felicitatem humanam, quae est ultimus finis, qualiscumque intelligibilis cognitio, nisi divina cognitio adsit, quae terminat naturale desiderium sicut ultimus finis. Est igitur ultimus finis hominis ipsa Dei cognitio." Thomas proves that God is the cause of all things in SCG II, 15.

In SCG III, 38 Thomas begins to specify the kind of knowledge that is meant. There he rejects the claim that happiness consists in the knowledge of God that is commonly had by the many. All men, Thomas notes, possess a certain general and confused knowledge of God. For the orderliness and regularity of nature leads most human beings to infer that there is a God who is the cause of all things. However, such a knowledge cannot constitute man's happiness, since it is imperfect (i.e., it is mixed with many errors), it is present in all almost from the very beginning of their lives, and an individual is blamed for lacking it. By contrast, happiness is a perfect knowledge, it is an end of human life, and no one is blamed for not having it.

In c. 39 Thomas rejects the claim that happiness consists in the knowledge of God that may be obtained through demonstration. While this mode of knowledge is superior to the knowledge had by the many, it is still imperfect. For by demonstration we come to know not what God is, but rather what he is not, and although this helps us to know how God is distinct from other things, it leaves us ignorant about what God is in himself. Moreover, happiness is a good that can be obtained by all, yet only a few can arrive at scientific knowledge of God. A merely philosophical knowledge of God cannot satisfy man's natural desire to know.[9]

In c. 40 Thomas shows that happiness does not consist in the knowledge of God given by faith. The latter is superior to the knowledge of God by way of demonstration, since faith teaches many truths about God that are inaccessible to reason. However, faith is an imperfect form of knowing, since in the act of believing the intellect does not grasp the object of its assent. As Thomas himself puts it: "Our natural desire is put to rest by happiness, since it is our ultimate end. However, the knowledge of faith does not quiet our desire, but rather inflames it, because everyone desires

---

[9] SCG III, 39 (ed. Leonina Manualis, 264). Note in particular: "Illa igitur cognitio Dei essentialiter est ipsa felicitas, qua habita non restabit alicuius scibilis desideranda cognitio. Talis autem non est cognitio quam philosophi per demonstrationes de Deo habere potuerunt: quia adhuc, illa cognitione habita, alia desideramus scire, quae per hanc cognitionem nondum sciuntur. Non est igitur in tali cognitione Dei felicitas."

to see what he believes. Therefore, the ultimate happiness of man is not found in the knowledge of faith."[10]

Thomas also denies that human happiness consists in the knowledge of God that is had by knowing the essences of separate substances. What he has in mind of course is the kind of knowledge that an angel has of God: an angel knows God by knowing its own essence; this is to know God in a more noble way than does a human being, since angels are more like God than we are. Nevertheless, in this life we do not know the essences of separate substances; our intellects are restricted to knowing the essences of material things.[11]

From the fact that in the present life we cannot grasp the essences of separate substances, Thomas infers that in this life we cannot see the divine essence.[12] Furthermore, since human happiness consists in the vision of the divine essence, it follows that happiness cannot be achieved in this life. Man's nature desire to know is never satisfied in the present life:

> the ultimate end of man terminates his natural appetite in such a way that, when it is obtained, he seeks nothing else.... But this is not possible in this life. For the more someone under-stands, the more the desire to understand, which is natural to man, is increased in him, unless perhaps he is someone who understands all things. But this has never happened to anyone in this life who was only a man, nor is it possible to happen, since in this life we cannot know separate substances, which are in the greatest degree intelligible.... Therefore, it is not possible that the ultimate happiness of man be in this life.[13]

---

[10] SCG III.40 (ed. Leonina Manualis, 265). "Per felicitatem, cum sit ultimus finis, nat-urale desiderium quietatur. Cognitio autem fidei non quietat desiderium, sed magis ipsum accendit: quia unusquisque desiderat videre quod credit. Non est igitur in cognitione fidei ultima hominis felicitas."

[11] SCG III.41-6. For another text in which Thomas denies to man in the present life a quidditative knowledge of separate substances, see *De Trin.* 6.3.

[12] SCG III, 47.

[13] SCG III, 48 (ed. Leonina Manualis, 277): "Ultimus finis hominis terminat eius appetitum naturalem, ita quod, eo habito, nihil aliud quaeritur.... Hoc autem in hac vita non est possibile accidere. Quanto enim plus aliquis intelligit, tanto magis in eo desideri-um intelligendi augetur, quod est hominibus naturale: nisi forte aliquis sit qui omnia intel-ligat. Quod in hac vita nulli unquam accidit qui esset solum homo, nec est possibile accidere: cum in hac vita substantias separatas, quae sunt maxime intelligibilia, cognoscere non possimus.... Non est igitur possibile ultimam hominis felicitatem in hac vita esse."

Moreover, happiness is a perfect good incompatible with any evil. But man's life on earth is never free from evils, whether of the body (hunger, thirst, etc.) or of the soul (ignorance, passion, etc.). Any good that is obtained in this life is lost in death.[14]

Granted that happiness is not achievable in the present life, Thomas reasons that human beings would have been created in vain if they were unable to acquire it:

> It is impossible that a natural desire be empty, 'for nature does nothing in vain' [*De caelo* II, 11, 291b]. But a natural desire would be empty if it never could be filled. Therefore, the natural desire of man is capable of being filled. But not in this life, as has been shown; therefore, it is necessary that it should be filled after this life. Therefore, the ultimate happiness of man is after this life.[15]

Since a natural desire cannot be in vain, happiness must be obtained after this life, when the human intellect will be elevated by divine grace to see the divine essence.[16]

In reaching this conclusion Thomas clearly has moved beyond the thought of Aristotle. The latter agrees that happiness is found in intellectual activity, but never suggests that it is not enjoyed in the present life or that it cannot be achieved by man's natural powers. Nevertheless, Thomas does not advance an otherworldly conception of happiness merely because it is required by Christian faith; it is by philosophical analysis that he concludes that man's ultimate end is the vision of God. Aristotle failed to arrive at this conclusion, not because he was a pagan, but because of the incomplete character of his philosophical account of happiness.

One finds a similar path of argumentation in the *Summa Theologiae* (1265-73). In ST I, 12 Thomas examines the manner in which God is

---

[14] Ibid.

[15] SCG III, 48 (ed. Leonina Manualis, 278): "Impossibile est naturale desiderium esse inane: *natura enim nihil facit frustra* [II de Caelo, XI; 291b]. Esset autem inane desiderium naturae si nunquam posset imperi. Est igitur implebile desiderium naturale hominis. Non autem in hac vita, ut ostensum est. Oportet igitur quod impleatur post hanc vitam. Est igitur felicitas ultima hominis post hanc vitam."

[16] Thomas gives an account of the mode of this knowing in SCG III, 51-3.

known by creatures. In a. 1 he establishes that the created intellect is able to see the divine essence. Because a thing is knowable insofar as it is in a state of actuality, God as pure act is maximally knowable (*maxime cognoscibile*). Yet the human mind is related to the most intelligible objects as the eyes of bats to the light of the sun. This has led some thinkers to conclude that human beings cannot see the divine essence. Thomas himself, however, strongly rejects this inference:

> Since the ultimate happiness of man consists in his highest activity, which is intellectual activity, if the created intellect can never see the essence of God, then either it never will obtain happiness, or its happiness consists in something other than God. But this is contrary to faith. For the ultimate perfection of a rational creature is in God, because he is the principle of its being, since a thing is perfect to the extent that it attains its principle. Similarly, it is contrary to reason. For there is in man a natural desire to know the cause, when he sees an effect, and from this wonder arises in men. Therefore, if the intellect of the rational creature is not able to arrive at the first cause of things, its natural desire will be in vain. Hence it must be conceded absolutely that the blessed see the essence of God.[17]

In this text Thomas asserts that human happiness is found in the vision of the divine essence. The denial that man can achieve this vision entails the denial of the possibility of human happiness, and is contrary to both faith and reason. Thomas offers a *philosophical* argument, based on the nature of man, to show that happiness (the vision of the divine essence) can be attained by man.

A more thorough treatment of human happiness is reserved for the opening questions of the *Prima Secundae*. In q. 1 Thomas analyzes man's ultimate end: a. 1 establishes that human beings act for the sake of an end;

---

[17] ST I, 12.1: "Cum enim ultima hominis beatitudo in altissima eius operatione consistat, quae est operatio intellectus, si nunquam essentiam Dei videre potest intellectus creatus, vel nunquam beatitudinem obtinebit, vel in alio eius beatitudo consistet quam in Deo. Quod est alienum a fide. In ipso enim est ultima perfectio rationalis creaturae, quod est ei principium essendi: intantum enim unumquodque perfectum est, inquantum ad suum principium attingit. Similiter etiam est praeter rationem. Inest enim homini naturale desiderium cognoscendi causam, cum intuetur effectum; et ex hoc admiratio in hominibus consurgit. Si igitur intellectus rationalis creaturae pertingere non possit ad primam causam rerum, remanebit inane desiderium naturae. Unde simpliciter concedendum est quod beati Dei essentiam videant."

a. 4 shows that there is an ultimate end for human life, which is demonstrated from the impossibility of an infinite regress in final causes. In a. 5 it is shown that one man cannot have many ultimate ends. Thomas first argument is especially worthy of note:

> since anything desires its own perfection, an individual desires as his ultimate end that which he desires as his perfect and complete good ...Therefore, it is necessary that the ultimate end should so fill man's entire appetite that there remains nothing outside of it to be desired. But this cannot be the case if something extraneous to its perfection is sought. Whence it cannot be the case that man's appetite tends towards two ultimate ends, as if each were his perfect good.[18]

Central to Thomas' understanding of an ultimate end is the notion that it must put to rest all human desire. The ultimate end must be a *perfect* good. If there were *two* perfect goods, each would differ from the other, and hence each would lack some degree of goodness that other possesses; therefore, neither could truly be thought of as a perfect good.

Thomas is careful also to distinguish two different ways of speaking about happiness: one may take it to mean that in which happiness is found, or it can refer to the attainment (*adeptio*), possession (*possessio*), or enjoyment (*usus, fruitio*) of that good.[19] The former is treated at some length in q. 2. Like Aristotle, Thomas is aware of the disagreement among the many concerning the object of happiness. In aa. 1-4 he rejects the claim that happiness is located in any of the external goods; in a. 5 that it is found in a corporeal good; in a. 6 in pleasure; in a. 7 in a good of the soul. His discussion reaches its climax in a. 8, which argues that happiness is found only in God:

> it is impossible that the happiness of man be found in some created good. For happiness is a perfect good, which completely satisfies desire; otherwise, it would not be the ultimate

---

[18] ST I-II, 1.5: "cum unumquodque appetat suam perfectionem, illud appetit aliquis ut ultimum finem, quod appetit ut bonum perfectum et completivum sui ipsius.... Oportet igitur quod ultimus finis ita impleat totum hominis appetitum, quod nihil extra ipsum appetendum relinquatur. Quod esse non potest, si aliquid extraneum ad ipsius perfectionem requiratur. Unde non potest esse quod in duo sic tendat appetitus, ac si utrumque sit bonum perfectum ipsius."

[19] ST I-II, 1.8.

> end if there still remained something to be desired. But the
> object of the will, which is human desire, is the universal good,
> just as the object of the intellect is universal truth. From this it
> is clear that only the universal good can satisfy the will of man.
> This is found not in some created good, but in God alone,
> because every creature has a participated goodness. Whence
> only God can fill the will of man.... Therefore, human happi-
> ness consists in God alone.[20]

The human will can be satisfied only by a perfect, unlimited good. Since
any created good merely participates its goodness, i.e., it has goodness
only in a limited, determinate way, no created good can satisfy completely the dynamism of the human will.

In q. 3 Thomas examines the essence of happiness more closely. Like
Aristotle, he regards it as an activity. However, he moves beyond the
Stagirite by distinguishing between perfect and imperfect happiness.
Since happiness denotes a certain ultimate perfection, it is said in different ways insofar as those beings capable of happiness can obtain diverse
levels of perfection. Happiness is in God essentially, since his being is
his activity. In angels happiness is an ultimate perfection in accordance
with that activity whereby they are joined to an uncreated good. In them
this activity is one and everlasting. However, for man in his present state,
the activity whereby he is joined to an uncreated good is not everlasting,
nor can it be continuous, and consequently, it is not one, because activity
is multiplied by its interruption. And so in the present life perfect happiness cannot be had by man. On this note Thomas cites Aristotle, who,
positing happiness to be in this life, called it imperfect, and later con-

---

[20] ST I-II, 2.8: "Impossibile est beatitudinem hominis esse in aliquo bono creato.
Beatitudo enim est bonum perfectum, quod totaliter quietat appetitum: alioquin non esset
ultimus finis, si adhuc restaret aliquid appetendum. Obiectum autem voluntatis, quae est
appetitus humanus, est universale bonum; sicut obiectum intellectus est universale verum.
Ex quo patet quod nihil potest quietare voluntatem hominis, nisi bonum universale. Quod
non invenitur in aliquo creato, sed solum in Deo: quia omnis creatura habet bonitatem par-
ticipatam. Unde solus Deus voluntatem hominis implere potest.... In solo igitur Deo beatitudo hominis consistit."

cluded "we call men happy, but as men." By contrast, Thomas observes, God has promised us complete happiness, when "we will be as the angels in heaven."[21]

Thomas also moves beyond Aristotle when he rejects the claim that happiness is found in the study of the theoretical sciences. In ST I-II, 3.6 Thomas reasons that the consideration of the theoretical sciences does not extend beyond the power of the principles of those sciences, since the whole of a science is contained virtually in its principles. Now the first principles of the theoretical sciences are grasped by way of the senses. Therefore, the consideration of the theoretical sciences cannot extend beyond what the knowledge of sensibles can reveal. Yet the ultimate perfection of the human intellect is found in the knowledge of something superior to it. But the knowledge of separate substances, which are superior to the human intellect, cannot be obtained by means of a knowledge of sensible things. Therefore, perfect happiness does not consist in the study of the theoretical sciences.

Finally, in ST I-II 3.8, Thomas establishes that man's ultimate happiness can be found only in a vision of the divine essence. His argument begins with two assertions: first, man is not perfectly happy as long as there remains some good for him to desire and seek; second, the perfection of any potency is judged in accordance with the nature of its object. Thomas then points out that the object of the intellect is the essence (*quod quid est*) of a thing; hence the intellect reaches its perfection when it knows what a thing is. Now if the knowledge of an effect is not able to reveal the essence of its cause, such that through the effect the intellect

---

21 ST I-II, 3.2.4: "Cum beatitudo dicat quandam ultimam perfectionem, secundum quod diversae res beatitudinis capaces ad diversos gradus perfectionis pertingere possunt, secundum hoc necesse est quod diversimode beatitudo dicatur. Nam in Deo est beatitudo per essentiam: quia ipsum esse eius est operatio eius, qua non fruitur alio, sed seipso. In angelis autem beatis est ultima perfectio secundum aliquam operationem, qua coniunguntur bono increato: et haec operatio in eis est unica et sempiterna. In hominibus autem, secundum statum praesentis vitae, est ultima perfectio secundum operationem qua homo coniungitur Deo: sed haec operatio nec continua potest esse, et per consequens nec unica est, quia operatio intercisione multiplicatur. Et propter hoc in statu praesentis vitae, perfecta beatitudo ab homine haberi non potest. Unde Philosophus, in *I Ethic.*, ponens beatitudinem hominis in hac vita, dicit eam imperfectam, post multa concludens: *Beatos autem dicimus ut homines*. Sed promittitur nobis a Deo beatitudo perfecta, quando erimus *sicut angeli in caelo*, sicut dicitur Mt. 22:30." For the text of Aristotle, see 1101a20.

knows of the cause *that it is* but not *what it is*, it is not said to grasp the cause absolutely (*simpliciter*). In this case the desire to know the cause remains. However, this is precisely how the human mind stands in relation to God. One knows that God is, but not what he is. Since all human beings desire to know, and knowledge is an understanding of causes, human beings naturally desire to know causes. Now when one knows that there exists a cause, one naturally desires to know its essence. And so Thomas concludes that man's perfect happiness requires a knowledge of the essence of the First Cause. Thus the human intellect achieves its full perfection only through a vision of God's essence.[22]

The texts that we have examined, from both the *Summa Contra Gentiles* and the *Summa Theologiae*, have a thoroughly rational character. Grounding his argument on the rational nature of human beings, Thomas shows that the ultimate end for man can be found only in a vision of the divine essence. Thomas' argument appears to be a rigorous philosophical deduction from the Aristotelian principle that all men naturally desire to know. As is well-known, this principle is the opening sentence of *Metaphysics* I.1. There Aristotle takes it as a basic claim about human nature; he makes no attempt to prove the claim, but instead offers a sign of its truth, namely, the delight that all human beings take in the senses, especially sight. It is interesting to note that in his Commentary on the *Metaphysics* (1271-2), Thomas offers three reasons to support the Aristotelian claim. Of these three it is the last argument that is the most interesting:

[22] ST I-II, 3.8. Note in particular: "ultima et perfecta beatitudo non potest esse nisi in visione divinae essentiae. Ad cuius evidentiam, duo consideranda sunt. Primo quidem, quod homo non est perfecte beatus, quandiu restat sibi aliquid desiderandum et quaerendum. Secundum est, quod uniuscuiusque potentiae perfectio attenditur secundum rationem sui obiecti. Obiectum autem intellectus est quod quid est, idest essentia rei.... Si ergo intellectus aliquis cognoscat essentiam alicuius effectus, per quam non possit cognosci essentia causae, ut scilicet sciatur de causa quid est; non dicitur intellectus attingere ad causam simpliciter, quamvis per effectum cognoscere possit de causa an sit. Et ideo remanet naturaliter homini desiderium cum cognoscit effectum, et scit cum habere causam, ut etiam sciat de causa quid est...Si igitur intellectus humanus, cognoscens essentiam alicuius effectus creati, non cognoscat de Deo nisi an est; nondum perfectio eius attingit simpliciter ad causam primam, sed remanet ei adhuc naturale desiderium inquirendi causam. Unde nondum est perfecte beatus. Ad perfectam igitur beatitudinem requiritur quod intellectus pertingat ad ipsam essentiam primae causae."

it is desirable for anything to be joined to its principle, for in
this the perfection of anything consists. Thus it is that circular
motion is the most perfect motion, as Aristotle proves in *Phy.*
VIII., because its ending point is joined to its starting point.
But man is joined to separate substances, which are principles
of the human intellect, and to which the human intellect is
related as the imperfect to the perfect, only by means of his
intellect. Thus it is in this that the ultimate happiness of man
is found. Therefore, man naturally desires knowledge.[23]

Thomas reasons that all things desire to be united with their "principle,"
i.e., their cause. Separate substances, i.e., immaterial beings (note that
Thomas does not tell us whether he means finite or infinite beings—
though he holds that only an infinite being is the cause of all things) are
the causes of material things. Thus human beings desire to be united to
God. But man, a material being, can be united with an immaterial being
only by his intellect, an immaterial power. One should recall that for
Thomas the intellect through the process knowing becomes its object, i.e.,
it becomes conformed to its object. And so the natural desire to know
coincides with the natural desire that man has to be united with his cause.
Philosophical reflection on the rational nature of human beings reveals
the naturalness of the vision of God. The philosopher, relying upon unaid-
ed reason, would seem to be able to arrive at a knowledge of what constitutes the ultimate perfection of man.

II

Nevertheless, one also finds a series of texts in which Thomas asserts
that faith is required for human beings to become aware of their destiny.
Thus without faith man would not know his ultimate end. This would
seem to entail a denial of any natural desire on the part of man to see God;
the vision is not man's natural end, but rather his supernatural end.

---

[23] *In I Meta.* lect 1, n. 4 (Marietti ed., 6): "quia unicuique rei desiderabile est, ut suo
principio conjungatur; in hoc enim uniuscujusque perfectio consistit. Unde et motus cir-
cularis est perfectissimus, ut probatur octavo Physicorum, quia finem conjungit principio.
Substantiis autem separatis, quae sunt principia intellectus humani, et ad quae intellectus
humanus se habet ut imperfectum ad perfectum, non conjungitur homo nisi per intellectum: unde et in hoc ultima hominis felicitas consistit. Et ideo naturaliter homo desiderat
scientiam."

One finds an early statement of this view in Thomas' Commentary on the *Sentences* (1252-6). In *II. Sent.* 29.1.1, Thomas emphasizes the need for grace, even for an individual in a state of innocence. Without grace, Thomas argues, one cannot obtain eternal life, since it is an end that exceeds the abilities of human nature, surpassing both the intellect and the desire of man. In support of this Thomas cites Paul's First Letter to the Corinthians ("The eye has not seen, the ears have not heard, and it has not entered the human heart, what God has prepared for those who love him").[24] This same claim is reiterated at *III Sent.* 23.1.4.3. In this text Thomas defends the need for a set of virtues in addition to the intellectual and moral virtues. The need for the theological virtues is grounded on the supernatural character of man's ultimate end:

> in all things that act for the sake of an end there must be an inclination for the end, and, as it were, a certain beginning of the end, otherwise [these things] would never seek to attain it. Now the end to which the divine liberality has ordained or predestined man, namely the enjoyment of God himself, is elevated wholly above the ability of created nature, since 'the eye has not seen nor the ear heard, nor has it entered the heart of man, what God has prepared for those who love him,' as it is said in I Cor. 2.9. Whence through his own natural abilities man does not have sufficiently an inclination to that end; therefore, it is necessary that something be added to man through which he might have an inclination to that end, just as by nature he has an inclination for an end connatural to himself. These additions are called the theological virtues for three reasons. First, with respect to their object. Since the end to which we are ordered is God himself, the inclination which is required consists in an operation concerning God. Second, with respect to their cause. Just as that end is ordained for us not by our own nature but by God, so too God alone causes in us the inclination for that end...Third, with respect to the knowledge of nature. Since the end is above the knowledge of nature, the inclination to the end cannot be known by natural

---

[24] *II Sent.* 29.1.1 (Mandonnet, 740): "Secundum hoc dico quod homo ante peccatum gratia indigebat, quia sine gratia finem vitae aeternae nullo modo consequi potuisset; ad finem enim non pervenitur nisi per opera proportionate fini: vita autem aeterna est finis omnino naturae humanae facultatem excedens; unde etiam intellectum et desiderium superat, I Corinth., II: 'Oculus non vidit, et auris non audivit, et in cor hominis non acscendit quae praeparavit Deus iis qui diligent illum.'" For the Pauline text see I Cor. 2.9.

> reason, but by divine revelation. Therefore, they are called the-
> ological, because they are revealed to us in Scripture; whence
> the philosophers know nothing about them.[25]

God has ordained an end for man that he can neither understand nor
desire by his own natural abilities. The vision of God is totally inaccessible to philosophical reason; man requires grace if he is to desire his ultimate end.

These same claims are repeated in the *De veritate* (1256-9). In *De
ver.* 14.12 Thomas attempts to justify the Pauline definition of faith. In
the course of his discussion he distinguishes a twofold ultimate good for
man:

> One of which is proportionate to human nature, because his
> natural powers are sufficient to obtain it, and this is the happi-
> ness of which the philosophers have spoken…. the other is a
> good exceeding the proportion of human nature, because his
> natural powers are not sufficient to obtain it, or even to con-
> ceptualize or desire it. From divine liberality alone it is
> promised to man, [as one reads in] I Cor. 2.9: 'The eye has not
> seen, O God, without you, what you have prepared for those
> expecting you,' and this is eternal life.[26]

---

25 *III Sent.* 23.1.4.3 (Moos, 714-5): "in omnibus quae agunt propter finem oportet esse
inclinationem ad finem, et quasi quamdam inchoationem finis: alias nunquam operaren-
tur propter finem. Finis autem ad quem divina largitas hominem ordinavit vel praedesti-
navit, scilicet fruitio sui ipsius, est omnino supra facultatem naturae creatae elevatus; quia
'nec oculus vidit nec auris audivit, nec in cor hominis ascendit, quae praeparavit Deus
diligentibus se,' ut dicatur I Cor., II, 9. Unde per naturalia tantum homo non habet suffi-
cienter inclinationem in finem illum; et ideo oportet quod superaddatur homini aliquid per
quod habeat inclinationem in finem illum, sicut per naturalia habet inclinationem ad finem
sibi connaturalem; et ista superaddita dicuntur virtutes theologicae ex tribus. Primo quantum ad objectum; quia cum finis ad quem ordinate sumus, sit ipse Deus, inclination quae
praeexigitur, consitit in operatione quae est circa ipsum Deum. Secundo quantum ad
causam; quia sicut ille finis est a Deon obis ordinates non per naturam nostrum, ita inclinationem in finem operator in nobis solus Deus…Tertio quantum ad cognitionem naturae,
quia cum finis sit supra cognitionem naturae, inclination in finem non potest per rationem
naturalem cognosci, sed per revelationem divinam; et ideo dicuntur theologicae, quia divi-
no sermone sunt nobis manifestatae, unde philosophi nihil de eis cognoverunt."

26 *De ver.* 14.2 (Leonine ed. 22.2, 441): "quorum unum est proportionatum naturae
humanae quia ad ipsum obtinendum vires naturales sufficiunt, et hoc est felicitas de qua
philosophi locuti sunt…. Aliud est bonum hominis naturae humanae proportionem excedens quia ad ipsum obtinendum vires naturales non sufficiunt, nec etiam ad cognoscen-
dum vel desiderandum, sed ex sola divina liberalitate homini repromittitur, I Cor. II
'Oculus non vidit' etc., et hoc est vita aeterna."

Similarly, in *De ver.* 27.2 Thomas notes that things which are diverse in nature have diverse ends. He then distinguishes three things necessary for the attainment of an end, namely, a nature proportionate to the end, a natural desire for the end, and a movement towards the end. In the case of man, that end which is proportionate to his nature, for which he has a natural desire, and which he can achieve by his own natural powers, is the contemplation of divine things. Philosophers see in this end the ultimate happiness of man. However, in truth man is called to a different ultimate end, namely the vision of God:

> But there is an end which God has prepared for man, exceeding the proportion of human nature, namely, eternal life which consists in the vision of God's essence. This [end] exceeds the proportion of any created nature and is connatural to God alone. Therefore, it is necessary that something be given man through which not only he may achieve the end, or that his appetite may be inclined to that end, but also so that his nature may be elevated to a dignity befitting that end. And for this grace is given to him.[27]

A clear distinction is drawn between man's ultimate end as posited by the philosophers and the end which is ordained for him by God. The latter is wholly supernatural. There is nothing in man's nature which enables him to achieve this end, or even to desire it; only God is able to raise man to this end.

In ST I, 1.1, Thomas argues that philosophy alone is insufficient for the conduct of human life; human beings have a need of sacred doctrine (*sacra doctrina*) if they are to achieve their ultimate end. Since man is ordered to God as to an end that exceeds the comprehension of his rea-

---

[27] *De ver.* 27.2 (Leonine ed. 22.3, 794): "Sed est aliquis finis ad quem homo a Deo praeparatur, naturae humanae proportionem excedens, scilicet vita aeterna quae consistit in visione Dei per essentiam, quae excedit proportionem cuiuslibet naturae creatae soli Deo connaturalis existens. Unde oportet quod homini detur aliquid non solum per quod operetur ad finem, vel per quod inclinetur eius appetitus in finem illum, sed etiam per quod ipsa natura hominis elevetur ad quandam dignitatem, secundum quam talis finis sit ei competens; et ad hoc datur gratia."

son, if he is to achieve salvation, his end must be made known to him, so that he may order his thoughts and actions to achieve it.[28]

Somewhat later at ST I-II, 114.2, in examining whether an individual without grace can merit eternal life, Thomas repeats the claim that human beings require grace if they are to know and desire their ultimate end:

> Eternal life is a good exceeding the proportion of created nature, because it surpasses even its knowledge and desire, according to I Cor. 2.9, 'the eye has not seen, nor the ear heard, nor has it entered the heart of man.' And so it is that no created nature is a sufficient principle of an act deserving of eternal life, unless there is added the supernatural gift which is called grace.[29]

One also finds this teaching in Thomas' later texts. In *De malo* 5.3 (1269-71), he asks whether infants who die in a state of original sin suffer the torments of spiritual pain. This is a theological problem, to be sure, but it it offers Thomas the occasion once more to contrast man's purely natural knowledge of his ultimate end with the knowledge that he obtains through faith. On the assumption that infants who die without baptism are able to engage in rational activity, the knowledge that they possess must be purely natural. One might wonder whether their lack of the beatific vision causes them any spiritual torment. Thomas himself prefers the view that such infants do not suffer spiritual torment. He notes that some hold this view because such infants die in a state of ignorance, not knowing that they were made for the vision of God. Others maintain that such infants lack the disorder of the will necessary to suffer spiritual torment. Thomas attempts to chart a middle course between these two views. Infants who die without baptism do not lack natural knowledge, but only supernatural knowledge, which accrues to one by faith:

[28] ST I, 1.1. Note in particular: "quia homo ordinatur ad Deum sicut ad quendam finem qui comprehensionem rationis excedit.... Finem autem oportet esse praecognitum hominibus, qui suas intentiones et actiones debent ordinare in finem. Unde necessarium fuit homini ad salutem, quod ei nota fierent quaedam per revelationem divinam, quae rationem humanam excedunt."

[29] ST I-II, 114.2: "Vita autem aeterna est quoddam bonum excedens proportionem naturae creatae: quia etiam excedit cognitionem et desiderium eius, secundum illud I ad Cor. 2,9: *Nec oculus vidit, nec auris audivit, nec in cor hominis ascendit.* Et inde est quod nulla natura creata est sufficiens principium actus meritorii vitae aeternae, nisi superaddatur aliquod supernaturale donum, quod gratia dicitur."

it belongs to its natural knowledge that the soul knows that it was created for the sake of happiness, and that its happiness consists in the attainment of the perfect good. But that the perfect good for which man was made is that glory which the saints possess, is beyond its natural knowledge. Whence the Apostle says in I Cor. 2.9 that 'the eye has not seen nor the ears heard nor has it entered the heart of man what God has proposed for those who love him,' and later he adds, 'But God revealed this to us through his Spirit.' This revelation belongs to faith.[30]

If man can know philosophically that his ultimate end is happiness, and that happiness consists in the attainment of the perfect good, it would seem that he cannot know that this perfect good is that enjoyed by the saints in heaven. Once again Thomas seems to deny that human beings could ever have a merely natural desire for the vision of God.

III

As we have seen, there is a tension in Thomas' texts on human destiny. In some texts he speaks of a natural desire in human beings for the vision of God; in other texts he denies the naturalness of this desire, attributing it instead to the effects of grace on the soul. This apparent inconsistency in Thomas' teaching has often troubled his commentators. One historically influential attempt to harmonize Thomas' position was made by Thomas de Vio (1468-1534), better known to us as Cajetan. The latter explained man's desire for the vision of God by appealing to the notion of an obediential potency. As understood by Aquinas, an obediential potency is a potency on the part of the creature to receive the supernatural action of God. For Cajetan the desire for the beatific vision is

---

[30] *De Malo* 5.3 (Leonine ed. 23, 136): "Pertinet autem ad naturalem cognitionem quod anima sciat se propter beatitudinem creatam, et quod beatitudo consistit in adeptione perfecti boni. Set quod illud bonum perfectum ad quod homo factus est, sit illa gloria quam sancti possident, est supra cognitionem naturalem. Unde Apostolus dicit I ad Cor. II quod 'nec oculus uidit nec auris audiuit nec in cor hominis ascendit, que preparauit Deus diligentibus se', et postea subdit 'Nobis autem reuelauit Deus per Spiritum suum'. Que quidem reuelatio ad fidem pertinet."

elicited only by the action of God upon the soul.[31] Since nature does not bestow an inclination for something that cannot be obtained by a natural power, man has the desire for the beatific vision only after he has been taught about this good by faith:

> the rational creature can be considered in two ways: in one way *absolutely*, in another way *as it is ordered to its happiness*. If it is considered in the first way, then its natural desire does not extend beyond the ability of its nature; and thus I concede that not naturally does it desire the vision of God in himself absolutely. But if it is considered in the second way, then it desires naturally the vision of God: because, as such, it knows certain effects, say of grace and glory, whose cause is God.... But when effects are known, it is natural for any intellectual substance to desire knowledge of the cause. And so the desire of the vision of God, though it is not natural to a created intellect absolutely, still it is natural to it, assuming the revelation of certain effects.[32]

On Cajetan's interpretation of Thomas, the beatific vision of God would constitute merely a supernatural end of man. Considered in itself, human nature does not have a natural inclination for the vision of God, since it cannot obtain this vision by its own efforts. However, it can be acted upon by God and receive his grace; by means of an obediential potency, it can desire the vision of the divine essence. Consequently, only an intellect informed by faith could know and desire this vision.

Nevertheless, Cajetan's interpretation cannot do justice to Thomas' repeated claims that human beings do have a natural desire for the vision

---

31 Cf. ST I, 1.1, *Commentaria Card. Caietani*, n. IX (Leonine ed. IV, 116): "vocatur autem potentia obedientialis, aptitudo rei ad hoc ut in ea fiat quidquid faciendum ordinaverit Deus. Et secundum talem potentiam, anima nostra dicitur in potentia ad beatitudinem pollicitam, et finem supernaturalem."

32 ST I, 12.1, *Commentaria Card. Caietani*, n. X (Leonine ed., IV, 116): "creatura rationalis potest dupliciter considerari: uno modo *absolute*, alio modo *ut ordinata est ad felicitatem*. Si primo modo consideretur, sic naturale eius desiderium non se extendit ultra naturae facultatem: et sic concedo quod non naturaliter desiderat visionem Dei in se absolute. Si vero secundo modo consideretur, sic naturaliter desiderat visionem Dei: quia, ut sic, novit quosdam effectus, puta gratiae et gloriae, quorum causa est Deus.... Notis autem effectibus, naturale est cuilibet intellectuali desiderare notitiam causae. Et proterea desiderium visionis divinae, etsi non sit naturale intellectui creato absolute, est tamen naturale ei, supposita revelatione talium effectuum."

of God. As we have seen, in both SCG III and ST I-II, 3.8 Thomas emphasizes that only the vision of God constitutes the perfect good of an intellectual substance. His arguments are deeply philosophical, resting on the intellectual dynamism at the heart of a rational nature.

Thomas clearly rejects the claim that any nature can have two ulti-mate ends. Man has only one ultimate end, namely the vision of the divine essence. Nevertheless, he does distinguish between man's imper-fect and his perfect happiness. The former is proportionate to human nature, and can be achieved in the present life by his native faculties; the latter exceeds the proportion of human nature, and is achievable only in the next life through the grace of God. One might wonder, however, about the precise relationship between imperfect and perfect happiness. Do they constitute two distinct ultimate ends for human nature?

For Aquinas imperfect happiness, as described by Aristotle, is radi-cally incomplete. The goodness that it possesses is partial, and ultimate-ly fails to satisfy the desire of human nature. By contrast, perfect happi-ness represents man's complete good; once it is attained there is nothing left for him to desire. Imperfect happiness, therefore, is happiness only in a qualified sense; strictly speaking, it ought not to be called happiness at all.

That the perfect good for man is not found in the present life is one of the central truths taught by Christianity. Yet for Aquinas it is also a truth accessible to the philosopher. At times he seems to attribute such an awareness to Aristotle. While acknowledging that in the *Nicomachean Ethics* Aristotle spoke only about happiness in the present life, Thomas points out that the Stagirite regards such happiness to be a qualified hap-piness:

> but because Aristotle saw that there is no other knowledge for
> man in this life than that of the speculative sciences, he posit-
> ed that man does not attain perfect happiness, but rather [hap-
> piness] in his own way.[33]

---

[33] SCG III, 48 (ed. Leonina manualis, 279): "quia vero Aristoteles vidit quod non est alia cognitio hominis in hac vita quam per scientias speculativas, posuit hominem non consequi felicitatem perfectam, sed suo modo."

Thomas reads Aristotle as understanding the limited character of the speculative sciences and their ultimate inability to put to rest man's boundless desire to know. He has in mind Aristotle's remark at 1101a20, that "we shall call happy those among living men in whom these conditions are, and are to be, fulfilled—but happy *men*."[34] Commenting on this text, Thomas observes that because it is difficult for individuals to satisfy all the conditions required for happiness, Aristotle adds that "we call such men happy, but as men, who, subject to the vicissitudes of this life, cannot have perfect happiness. And because the desire of nature cannot be empty, rightly it can be judged that perfect happiness is reserved for man after this life.[35]

What is significant, of course, is that Thomas does seem to think that philosophers can have some awareness of what constitutes the perfect happiness for a human being. Such an awareness is quite vague and indistinct, and it is perhaps for this reason that Thomas often appeals to faith to assure man of his true destiny. One finds support for this in the opening chapters of the *Summa Contra Gentiles*. In SCG I, 3 Thomas makes an important distinction between two kinds of truths about God: some are wholly inaccessible to human reason (for example, propositions about the Trinity); others are able to be discovered by reason (such as, "God exists," God is one," etc.). For Thomas it was fitting for God to reveal both kinds of truths to human beings. If those truths about God that are accessible to reason were only rational and not able to be revealed (i.e., if our only access to these truths were through reason), then it would happen that only a few individuals would possess these truths, and that only after much time, and the knowledge of these individuals would be mingled with much falsehood.[36]

According to Thomas, SCG I-III deal with truths that are rationally accessible; it is not the case that they are grasped only by faith. His goal

---

[34] The Latin text used by Thomas reads: "Si ita autem, beatos dicemus viventium, quibus existunt et existent quae dicta sunt: beatos autem ut homines."

[35] In I Eth. lect. 16, n. 202 (Marietti ed., 53): "quod tales dicimus beatos sicut homines, qui in hac vita mutabilitati subiecti, non possunt perfectam beatitudinem habere. Et quia non est inane naturae desiderium, recte existimari potest, quod reservatur homini perfecta beatitudo post hanc vitam."

[36] SCG I, 4.

is to provide demonstrative reasons to convince an adversary of their truth. SCG IV, however, deals with truths are inaccessible to human reason. No demonstrative reasons can be given for these truths; one must be content to answer the arguments that an adversary brings against them.[37]

Consequently, the truths established about man's ultimate end in SCG III should be regarded as rationally accessible; it is not the case that that they are knowable to faith alone. That human happiness consists in the vision of God, and that this vision is the ultimate desire of human nature, are truths which are philosophically accessible. However, the philosopher's understanding of these truths is vague and indistinct. The philosopher can come to know that the desire of the will comes to rest only with the possession of a perfect good, and that no created good is a perfect good. From an analysis of human reason the philosopher can come to know that the intellect's desire comes to rest only with an understanding of the first cause. Although the philosopher can come to know where genuine happiness is found, this knowledge remains indistinct and vague. Faith provides a fuller teaching about God, and about the content of human destiny. Although reason can show that human happiness is found only in a vision of the divine essence, it cannot know that God actually grants this vision. The divine will is free, and it is not necessary that God will anything outside of himself. It is only by faith that human beings know that God does grant this vision.

Thomas himself is unaware of an inconsistency in his teaching on human happiness. One finds in his writings rational arguments to show that happiness is found only in the vision of God, and that human beings have a natural desire for this vision. These truths are philosophically accessible. At the same time, he is aware of the limited character of human reason. Only a small number of individuals are able to discover these truths merely by following reason. Philosophers themselves understand these truths in a partial and incomplete manner. By means of faith, however, these truths become accessible to all individuals. Faith offers a richer and more complete teaching on human destiny and is available to all. The apparent inconsistency of Thomas' texts, therefore, is due to the different perspectives from which human nature may be viewed. The theologian sees more than the philosopher, yet each sees truly.

[37] SCG I, 9.

DESCRIPTIVE PROCEDURAL ASPECTS OF AQUINAS'S NATURAL LAW THEORY
Polycarp Ikuenobe

INTRODUCTION

The major legal positivist's criticism of Aquinas's natural law theory comes from a narrow understanding of his endorsement of St. Augustine's statement: "that which is not just seems to be no law at all."[1] This understanding is underscored by Aquinas's statement: "Hence the force of a law depends on the extent of its justice."[2] These statements are understood as saying that if the content of a law is immoral or unjust, then it cannot be a valid law in any legal system; that is, the legal validity of law (understood as its binding force) depends on whether it is, in content, moral or just. For H. L. A. Hart, "the assertion that 'an unjust law is not a law' has the same ring of exaggeration and paradox, if not falsity as 'statutes are not laws' or 'constitutional law is not law'."[3] The legal positivist's stance is that Aquinas confuses the issue of legal obligation or the validity of a law, which involves having a criterion of identification or existence, with the issue of moral obligation or the moral adequacy of a law, which involves a determination of whether a law is just or not.[4] The issue of legal validity is descriptive while the issue of moral adequacy is normative. Legal positivists argue that a legal theory is supposed to provide a descriptive account and a conceptual analysis of law. What Aquinas's natural law theory provides, they argue, is a normative legal theory.

---

[1] Saint Thomas Aquinas, *The Summa Theologica*, in *Basic Writings of Saint Thomas Aquinas*, edited and Annotated, with an Introduction, by Anton C. Pegis (New York: Random House,1945), question 95, 2nd article, p.784 (will be cited subsequently as *Summa Theologica*).

[2] Ibid., question 95, 2nd article, p.784.

[3] H. L. A. Hart, *The Concept of Law*, 2nd edition (Oxford: Clarendon Press, 1997), p. 8.

[4] This is the sense in which J. L. Austin argues that: "The existence of law is one thing; its merit or demerit is another." Legal positivists criticize Aquinas for conflating these two.

This interpretation of Aquinas's natural law theory is parochial, in that it fails to fully appreciate other significant conceptual, descriptive, and procedural aspects of his view. Even a natural law theorist like Lon Fuller distinguishes between his view, which he sees as procedural, from the classical view of Aquinas, which is said to be normative and content-based.[5] Russell Hittinger acknowledges that "Fuller's natural law theory affirmed a 'natural law concerned with procedures' rather than a traditional one of 'substantive ends'."[6] This implies that there are two plausible ways of construing natural law theory. The procedural account, which is attributed to Lon Fuller, is usually contrasted with the substantive moral end or content account, which is attributed to Aquinas. In this paper, I examine Aquinas's natural law theory in order to attempt a 'reinterpretation' of his account of law. I do not offer a coherent comprehensive account of his natural law theory that places his view in the context of his theology and metaphysics. I argue that his theory of law must be seen as both a descriptive procedural and substantive content or end view of the nature of law. If Aquinas's theory is so construed, then it may be able to deflect some criticisms. So, the thrust of my stance is to offer a hypothesis regarding how Aquinas's natural law theory may be understood in the contexts of the natural law tradition, modern jurisprudential debates, and the different but related tasks that he sought to achieve. These tasks include (1) an account of two essences or natures of law, which are normative and procedural; (2) an account of the 'core' and 'peripheral' senses of the concept of law; (3) a typology of law and their connections.

[5] Lon Fuller, *The Morality of Law* (New Haven: Yale University Press, 1964). This point is also acknowledged by John Finnis, *Natural Law and Natural Rights* (Oxford: Clarendon Press, 1980), p. 18, and Michael Baur, "Natural law, the Legislation of Virtue: Historicity, Positivity, and Circularity" *Vera Lex*, Vol 2, Nos 1&2, p. 54. Baur indicates "It is important to remember here that Aquinas's account of law is a normative account, and not merely a descriptive or empirical account."

[6] Russell Hittinger, "Natural Law and Virtue" in Robert P. George, ed., *Natural Law Theory: Contemporary Essays*, (Oxford: Clarendon Press, 1992), pp. 42-70, indicates that "Fuller's natural law theory affirmed a 'natural law concerned with procedures' rather than a traditional one of 'substantive ends'" (p. 69, note 37).

TWO ESSENCES OF LAW, AND THE NATURE OF MORAL AND LEGAL OBLIGATION

According to Aquinas's definition, "Law is nothing else than an ordinance of reason for the common good, promulgated by him who has the care of the community."⁷ Human laws are "particular determinations, devised by human reason, ... provided that the other essential conditions of law be observed, as was stated above."⁸ These essential conditions refer to the formal elements of law discussed in question 90 of *Summa*, which are summarized as follows: (1) an ordinance of reason, (2) for the common good, (3) promulgated, and (4) by him who has care of the community. According to Aquinas's definition, human law may be seen as having two different essences or natures. One involves the substantive moral content or end nature, and the other involves the descriptive procedural nature. Given these two natures, we must see his conceptual analysis of law in terms of the following key notions or concepts: 'he who has care of the community', 'reason', 'common good', and 'promulgate', which have both descriptive and normative connotations. His definition and conceptual analysis imply that in order for a human law to have the two essences of law, it must on the one hand be procedurally adequate, and on the other hand, it must be substantively just in content. A human law is morally adequate or just, if and only if, given adequate just and moral procedures, it has a just substantive content, which is properly framed using reason or it is correctly and rationally deduced from eternal law to serve the common good.⁹

Given this analysis, we must understand Aquinas as giving an account not only of the nature of 'a law' as a specific statute or set of statutes and their contents, but also the nature of a legal system as set of procedures for making and applying laws. Therefore, Aquinas cannot simply be understood as giving an account of the nature of the moral content and moral validity of laws. Such construal will be parochial: it fails to pay attention to the descriptive procedural aspects of his account of the nature of law. It is pertinent to note that Aquinas sought to do a number

⁷ *Summa Theologica*, op. cit., question 90, 4th article, p. 747.

⁸ Ibid., question 92, 3rd article, p. 751.

⁹ Ibid., question 93, 4th article, p. 766.

of things. In question 90 of *Summa*, he explores the *essence of law*, in terms of indicating the essential, or perhaps, necessary conditions that must exist in order for a precept to be characterized as a law. It is in this regard that he indicates the above four essential elements of law. In the first article of question 90, he argues that a law involves reason, in that it must be a universal proposition of practical reason, a principle of action, and a guide for conduct. According to him, "Law is a rule and measure of acts, whereby man is induced to act or is restrained from acting; for *lex* [law] is derived from *ligare* [to bind], because it binds one to act. Now the rule and measure of human acts is the reason, which is the first principle of human acts, as is evident from what has been stated above."[10] As propositions of practical reason, a law has the feature of being normative, in that it is a rule or a measure that provides a practically reasonable guide for conduct or action.

The idea that a law is a guide for conduct implies that it has a binding force, which means that the people who obey it consider it a precept that they legally or socially ought to obey. This indicates that it is valid as the socially *accepted* or *acceptable* standard for conduct. To use H. L. A Hart's terminology, it means that the people accept it from an internal point of view.[11] For Aquinas, the criterion for validity, identification, and existence of a law, involves the process by which it is promulgated and accepted as the law of the people. A precept is a law, which means it is procedurally valid, just in case it is promulgated, backed by punishment, and is able to create the inclination on the part of people to obey. Such validity is necessary for a precept to be a law with a binding force. A valid law that has the ability to engender "the inclination of the members to concupiscence is called *the law of the member*."[12] The validity of a law, i.e., the fact that it meets certain formal criteria, creates in some sense, the inclination on the part of people to obey. Such formal or descriptive procedural validity of a law, which may or may not involve substantive moral validity, indicates that a law may be called "the law of the mem-

10 Ibid., question 90, 1th article, p. 743.

11 H. L. A. Hart, *The Concept of Law* (Oxford: Clarendon Press, 1997), p. 89. He defines the internal point of view with respect to laws, as that of "members of the group which accepts and uses them as guides to conduct" as well as the standards for criticizing others' conduct.

12 *Summa Theologica*, op. cit., question 90, 1th article, p. 743.

ber," which means that the law is considered by members of a society to be a law. So, one descriptive procedural element of a valid law, involves *the fact* that it has coercive power, is backed by punishment or able to inflict penalties.

The coercive power of law derives, in part, from the fact that it is promulgated and its procedures are generally accepted by many people in the community. People obey law and recognize its coercive power because they accept the process of framing and promulgating a law as the criterion for its validity and the basis for its binding force. Aquinas indicates this point in the following: "But this coercive power is vested in the whole people or in some public personage, to whom it belongs to inflict penalties, ..."[13] In his view, punishment is an essential formal feature or the effect of law, and it can only come from someone who has the legitimate authority to administer the law.[14] He argues that "the notion of law contains two things: first, that it is a rule of human acts; secondly, that it has coercive powers."[15] Laws are the products of human actions based on practical reason; they are framed by people with the power and authority to make laws as reasonable means for achieving desired ends. The coercive power of the law creates its ability to train humans by compelling and proscribing certain conduct. In his words, "this kind of training, which compels through fear of punishment, is the discipline of laws."[16] The training in this case involves the ability to know the law, understand its coercive power, accept its implication in terms of punishment, and to use it as a guide for conduct. This criterion is a formal requirement for a law to engender the desire for obedience or its binding force—*ligare*. This is the sense in which, for Aquinas, the validity or binding force of a law derives, in part (at least formally and procedurally), from its promulgation.

To appreciate this formal, coercive, and procedural account of law as a basis for its binding force, we must understand Aquinas's discussion of the notion of 'promulgation of law' as one essential element of the validity criterion of a law. According to him, "in order that a law obtain the

13 Ibid., question 90, 3rd article, p. 746.

14 Ibid. question 92, 2nd article, p. 761.

15 Ibid., question 96, article 6, p. 796.

16 Ibid., question 95, 1st article, p. 783.

binding force which is proper to a law, it must needs be applied to the men who have to be ruled by it. But such application is made by its being made known to them by promulgation. Therefore, promulgation is necessary for law to obtain its force."[17] Here, Aquinas discusses two senses of 'promulgation' of law. The first involves the process of instilling natural law into the human mind or the process of making it known to humans via reason. This process is timeless and it continues from the present into future. The second involves the process of a legislator making known to subjects the laws they are bound to obey. This process is not timeless, in that it occurs in writing or by words of mouth at a particular time and place. He insists that "Those who are not present when a law is promulgated are bound to observe the law, in so far as it is made known or can be made known to them by others, after it has been promulgated."[18] This involves the idea that if a law is written then people can read it in order to ascertain its existence and validity. Thus, he indicates "that *lex [law] is derived from legere [to read] because it is written.*" So, the inclination to obey a law that one can ascertain comes from the fact that an accepted criterion of validity exists, and it has been promulgated in accordance with the formal process or criterion. These descriptive procedural facts about the nature of law are the basis for its binding force. This descriptive procedural account of promulgation, the validity of law, and its binding force does not have a normative content or end element.

In addition to the procedural and coercive natures of law, Aquinas also insists that a law may have substantive content nature that is moral or just. The distinction between the procedural and substantive content natures of law may help to illuminate his accounts of moral and legal obligation. For him, legal obligation is not equivalent to moral obligation. Moral obligation, which derives from the substantive moral content or end of law does not necessarily imply legal obligation and vice versa. One issue that has been raised by critics is whether Aquinas's idea of legal obligation necessarily derives from moral obligation. One legal positivist's criticism is that Aquinas's view implies that legal obligation always derives from moral obligation. But it is important to note that Aquinas does not offer his moral or normative view of legal validity or

17 Ibid., question 90, 4th article, p. 747.

18 Ibid., question 90, 4th article, p. 747.

the substantive moral content of a law as the descriptive procedural basis for what, in any community, the law is, or what it takes for the law to exist or to be identified as having a binding force and obeyed. Aquinas argues that "It is not always through the perfect goodness of virtue that one obeys the law, but sometimes it is through fear of punishment ..."[19] The perfect goodness of virtue is a conceptual essence of natural law, in virtue of which a law may bind in conscience and engender moral obligation. But such goodness as the basis for moral obligation is not a conceptual aspect of human law.

The precepts of natural law are substantively and procedurally good moral principles derived from human nature and reason, which specify how people ought to do things and relate to one another in order to maintain a peaceful and acceptable society. These precepts also involve how people may use law, via legal processes and substantive content, to promote common good and to avoid evil.[20] A law that is promulgated, which is essential for a precept to be a human law, has to be backed by coercive power. But natural law is not promulgated in the same sense in which human laws are promulgated and backed by force. So, the conceptual and procedural features of human law and legal obligation, which are not part of moral obligation, are promulgation and the coercive threat of punishment. Aquinas did emphasize that legal obligation that is associated with a law framed by humans based on reason is not equivalent to the moral obligation that is associated with the moral content of natural law; human law does not necessarily have a valid moral content because they could be just or unjust. Aquinas indicates that human law is fallible and subject to change, whereas natural law does not vary with time and circumstance.

Natural law is unchangeable in its first principles, but not in its secondary principles that involve the application of first principles to particular instances, such as in human law.[21] For Aquinas, "human law is rightly changed in so far as such change is conducive to the common welfare."[22] The idea of changing human law indicates that there are proce-

---

[19] Ibid., question 92, 1st article, p. 759.

[20] Ibid., question 94, 2nd article, pp. 774-5.

[21] Ibid., question 94, 5th article, p. 779.

[22] Ibid., question 97, 2nd article, p. 802.

dures for changing the content and procedures of law. This idea also indicates human fallibility. Fallibility indicates that we can improve human knowledge about the proper means and ends, which are then reflected in how to frame and promulgate law, as well as what is framed as the substantive content of a law. Hence, legal obligation regarding human law is essentially different from moral obligation with respect to natural law, because the former has the essential formal and descriptive procedural features of promulgation and coercive force, which the latter law lacks. Aquinas insists that the binding force of law in any community derives from its procedural essence, which involves the threat of punishment and the formal process of promulgation, irrespective of whether or not the law is moral or just. It does not matter whether or not a law is in content or end consistent with or accurately derived from eternal law via natural law. The validity of law and its ability to engender obedience is not based on its moral adequacy but whether or not the requisite procedures are properly followed. So, for Aquinas, the fact that a law is, in content, substantively just is neither a necessary nor a sufficient condition for legal validity, in terms of the ability of a law to have a binding force.

Aquinas distinguishes between a law that binds in conscience, which implies that it engenders moral obligation by being substantively just, and a law that binds legally and procedurally simply because it is promulgated and has coercive force. Aquinas indicates that a law that is substantively just has the power to bind in conscience, and the *power* to bind in conscience derives from eternal law, the moral exemplar from which human laws are rationally derived via natural law. The instantiation or exemplification of the exemplars of eternal law via reason in the nature of things, including the rational nature of human beings, constitutes natural law. And natural law needs to be translated, via human reason and understanding, into human law for the common good by a formal legislative process of promulgation by someone with legitimate authority. As an 'approximation' of natural law, human laws are adapted by people to suit their unique situations, based on what reason dictates in given circumstances, so that a society can achieve the goal of disciplining people and guiding their conduct for the common good.[23] Thus, a human law, in its

---

23 Ibid., question 95, 3rd article, p. 786.

substantive moral content or end, may or may not approximate the moral essence of natural law. "Human law has *the nature of law* in so far as it partakes in right reason; and it is clear that, in this respect, it is derived from the eternal law."[24] The idea that a human law has the ability to bind in conscience requires that it partakes in the right reason.

For Aquinas, "reason leads us from certain principles to assent to the conclusion, so it induces us by some means to assent to the precepts of law."[25] A law may be incorrectly deduced from eternal law, hence it may be unjust. One nature or normative aim of human law is to mirror the exemplar: the *ideal nature of law*. The *real nature of law*, which is instantiated in human law, is shaped by descriptive procedural factors which reflect human reality. Such reality is a function of time, custom, circumstance, reason, human knowledge, and understanding. The fact that the substantive content of a law is just, in that it is rationally derived from eternal law, is a normative but and only one sense in which a law is valid and binding.[26] This just content by itself alone may create a moral obligation to obey a law. Such just content does not by itself create legal obligation, because legal obligation also requires that a law be valid in a procedural sense. The fact that a law is, in content substantively just, and consistent with the common good, does not imply that it is procedurally valid and binding to require legal obligation. For instance, the procedures for making, promulgating, and applying a law may not be followed or may not be unacceptable even though the substantive ends and contents of the laws that derive from them are just. There may be a moral obligation to obey such laws solely because of their good moral content or end. Absent the proper procedural features, there may not be a legal obligation to obey such just and moral laws.

Being just, morally valid, or morally binding in the substantive content sense of partaking in reason and being derived from eternal law is only one nature–i.e., the normative essence of law. This normative essence of a law alone does not imply that it will bind in the legal sense. The power of a human law to bind legally is external, and hence it is not

24 Ibid., question 93, 4th article, p. 766.

25 Ibid., question 92, 2nd article, p. 760.

26 Ibid., question 96, 4th article, p. 794.

conceptually connected or internal to an individual's motivation or reasons for action and obeying the law. Aquinas indicates that many people have different reasons for obeying the law, which vary from its validity, promulgation, threat of punishment, its reasonableness, the need to live a life of virtue and peace, to a moral obligation arising from the perceived moral character of the law.[27] The moral obligation to obey a law arises solely from an internalist view that it is just or moral; hence, it binds in conscience and motivates a person to act. Aquinas provides internalist accounts of moral obligation and moral reasons for actions. Aquinas's account of moral obligation and moral reasons for actions indicates that the moral adequacy of a precept is logically tied to its ability to bind in conscience and motivate. This is not the case with legal obligation. Thus, he provides externalist accounts of an agent's legal obligation, motivation, legal reasons for action, and legal authority or power.

THE BASIS OF OBLIGATION AND THE 'CORE' AND 'PERIPHERAL' SENSES OF LAW

Aquinas account of reasons for action with respect to legal obligation is not internalist because he does not indicate that one is necessarily motivated to obey a law based solely on its moral content or end, in virtue of which it binds in conscience. The morality of a law is not internal to or logically linked to the legal reasons for action and the motivation to obey the law. Moreover, it is not necessarily the case that all laws that fail to bind in conscience are substantively unjust. The fact that a law does not bind in conscience may be due to the fact that someone has not rationally understood its moral end or connection with eternal law. Such understanding makes a law to bind in conscience and motivates rational people to obey. The fact that a precept is just may not by itself alone motivate lawmakers to frame or promulgate it as a law, and such a fact alone may not motivate people to obey a law. The fact that there is a moral obligation as a result of the justness of a precept, and the fact that it has the power to bind in conscience, do not necessarily imply that everyone will

27 Ibid., question 92, 1st article, p. 759. Aquinas argues that "It is not always through the perfect goodness of virtue that one obeys the law, but sometimes it is through fear of punishment, and sometimes from the mere dictate of reason, which is a beginning of virtue."

legally recognize it as creating a legal obligation; it may not have the procedural essence of law by being promulgated and being backed by the threat of punishment. This implies that the rational recognition of justice, one's moral obligation, or the mere ability to morally bind in conscience, may not necessarily motivate an agent (lawgiver or subject) or provide her legal reasons to act—to legislate or obey a law. Thus, moral obligation is not logically tied to legal obligation.

The legal reasons for action include external descriptive procedural legal factors. In order for a law to engender legal obligation, it must satisfy societal norms, legal procedures, and other descriptive features, which are external to its moral adequacy. A determination regarding the moral adequacy of a law will provide legal reasons and motivation for action, only in the context of practical reason, the community, its custom, and legal procedures. Thus, legal obligation does not necessarily derive from the moral adequacy of the content or end of a law or of its procedures. Legal obligation derives from the accepted procedures that reflect the custom of a community, on the basis of which the powers of lawgivers and legal processes are rationally created as the appropriate means. It is in virtue of these factors that the contents and ends of laws are framed, promulgated, backed by threat of punishment, applied, and obeyed. Contrary to some critics' suggestion, Aquinas did not conflate legal and moral obligation. A law must be procedurally valid, as opposed to being morally valid, in order to bind legally and to engender legal obligation. Such procedural validity is indicated by the act of promulgation by *him who has care of the community*. We must understand what he means by "him who has care of the community" in order to appreciate his notion of legal validity and his externalist view of legal obligation.

Aquinas's specification that a law is promulgated by "him who has care of the community" is purposely ambivalent, to indicate his view regarding the two natures of law. One valence of the notion of "him who has care of the community" involves *a description* of someone, a ruler, who has power or legitimate authority to *take care of* the community, and such authority derives from general acceptance by those who are subject to the laws. This person satisfies one of the procedural criteria for determining the validity of law, which indicates the formal pedigree or procedural source of a law. It also indicates the locus of the power to make law by specifying that a law must properly originate from such a source. The criterion for determining who has the power to make law is stated as follows: "the making of law belongs either to the whole people or to a public personage who has care of the whole people."[28] This suggests that the whole community is involved in the process of making law directly, or indirectly through representatives who constitute public personage. While the idea of 'whole people' cannot be understood literally as everyone in the community, it is reasonable to assume that he expects communities to have a set of generally accepted criteria, based on practical reason, their customs, and circumstances, for determining who can, either as a 'whole people' or 'public personage', be a legislator.

Aquinas alludes to this assumption by indicating that: "A law is an ordinance of the people, whereby something is sanctioned by the Elders together with the commonality. Therefore, not everyone can make laws."[29] So, lawmakers have the legal responsibility to make laws according to the proper procedure. This responsibility is not, as some people may want to understand Aquinas's view, solely a moral one, in terms of making sure that the substantive content of a law is just or moral. The legal responsibility to make laws derives from the powers and authority that the community gives to those who are deemed qualified to make laws. These laws are then deemed valid because they are made by the proper people by following the proper procedures and using the proper criteria. This legal responsibility implies that lawmakers must be guided by practical reason, in terms of using adequate means to achieve the requisite end of the common good. Common good, for Aquinas, may in one sense, be understood purely in moral terms of helping people to live a good life of virtue and self-preservation, which for Aquinas, is a natural human inclination that law should seek to enhance and preserve.

This moral sense of common good underscores the second valence of "him who has care of the community" which is normative. This implies that legislators or lawgivers must, in the substantive content of a law, indicate explicitly that they care about the welfare of those who are subject to laws. Such care is manifested in the justness of the substantive

---

[28] Ibid., question 90, 4th article, p. 746.

[29] Ibid., question 90, 3rd article, p. 745.

content of a law, and is constrained by the validity criteria and procedures of a legal system that require that a law must follow the proper procedures, which in an ideal case, must be moral. A legal procedure or law-making process is practically reasonable and moral if it is not tyrannical or if it forbids the abuse of power, so that the law can lead to the common good. This point is underscored by indicating that "All law proceeds from the reason and will of the lawgiver ... the human law from the will of man as regulated by reason."[30] Human law is a product of the *will* and *reason* of the lawgiver. By satisfying the two criteria or valences of 'care' and the descriptive procedural criterion of validity, a law is deemed to be an ordinance of reason, at least in the normative sense of being a reasonable means in the given context for achieving the end of the common good. For Aquinas, "in order that the volition of what is commanded may have *the nature of law*, it needs to be in accord with some rule of reason."[31] As an ordinance of reason, Aquinas may be understood as saying that in order to be categorized as a law, a precept must meet certain *content* and *procedural* standards of practical reason.

A law must have a practically reasonable set of procedures and a practically reasonable substantive content with respect to the substantive end of common good. A law can be for the common good in two different senses: a law can be for the common good in the first sense of being substantively normative or moral in content. A law can also be for the common good in the second sense of being general in a purely descriptive, procedural, or formal sense. While the normative sense of common good has a universal connotation, the descriptive sense of common good has a contingent connotation, which refers descriptively to the common, *general*, and *public* good of a particular society. As a reflection of this sense of common good, a law is not directed at private issues or interests or the needs of a few or particular people. A law is for the common good in a descriptive sense, just in case the law, as a prohibition, has elements of being general and public in its scope and application. This point is underscored the fact that Aquinas sees law as applying primarily to public matters and public safety. Aquinas also insists that "law does not pre-

---

30 Ibid., question 97, 3rd article, p. 803.

31 Ibid., question 90, 1st article, p. 744 (The emphasis on 'the nature of law' is mine. Here, Aquinas indicates that one nature of law is for it to be in accord with reason).

scribe all acts of virtue." Laws cannot prescribe virtues that pertain solely to individuals' private good; it only prescribes virtues that pertain to
the public good.[32] This does not imply that the public good may not be
conducive to the private good.

Aquinas argues that "human laws do not forbid all vices, ... but only
the more grievous vices, from which it is possible for the majority to
abstain; and chiefly those that are injurious to others, without the prohibition of which human society could not be maintained."[33] This seems to
indicate that being for the common good implies that a law is general or
public in the descriptive sense, and as such, common good is not necessarily synonymous with substantive morality. Law is not simply the legislation or application of moral principles or moral virtues, which are the
manifestations of the natural law. There is, for Aquinas, more to the
nature of law than its substantive moral or natural law content. As
Aquinas argues:

> Whatever is for an end should be proportioned to that end.
> Now the end of law is the common good, because ... law
> should be framed, not for any private benefit, but for the com-
> mon good of all citizens. Hence human laws should be pro-
> portioned to the common good. Now the common good com-
> prises many things. Therefore law should take account of
> many things, as to persons, as to matters, and as to times. For
> the community of the state is composed of many persons, and
> its good is procured by many actions; nor is it established to
> endure for only a short time, but to last for all time by the cit-
> izens succeeding one another as Augustine says.[34]

Common good is used here in a descriptive sense of having a general and public element, and in the sense of being a substantive moral end.
In these senses, a law has the ability to meet the needs and substantive
ends of a variety of people, with respect to a variety of issues or matters,
in a variety of circumstances, and in a variety of times, irrespective of the
moral character of those needs. This is one sense in which the common
good consists of many things.

[32] Ibid., question 96, 3rd article, p. 793.

[33] Ibid., question 96, 2nd article, p. 792.

[34] Ibid., question 96, 1st article, pp. 790-1.

Aquinas indicates that there must be a contingent public stricture and a generality constraint on what should count as law. The contingent stricture of common good, which is understood descriptively as indicating the public scope of the law or its publicity with respect to promulgation, is an essential nature of law. It is clear from the above passage that Aquinas is concerned about the nature of law as a legal system or a set of procedures that is enduring, and a set of substantive contents that is general, in the sense that the content of a law is applicable to everyone in different situations. Aquinas's analysis of the concept of 'law' must be seen in terms of a formal precept with a substantive content, which is properly derived from a system or a set of structures and procedures that humans have rationally devised as a set of means for achieving some particular goals or ends, including the common good. The procedural constraints of validity on laws may be viewed in terms of performing the function of indicating when a precept is to count as a law. Law is in many respects, for Aquinas, a functional concept. Therefore, an important element of his account of law is its function: achieving substantive ends. We may understand natural law as providing normative criteria in terms of reasonable procedural constraints and substantive moral constraints that must be placed on human law in order to attain the normative goal.

Because of the human use of practical reason in different circumstances, the formal processes of legislation vary from place to place. Natural law precepts, which represent principles of practical reason, indicate normatively, the morally acceptable formal procedures for promulgating a law, the proper authority of a lawgiver, and the normative criterion by which a law is deemed valid. Natural law precepts also indicate the normative criteria for determining the acceptable substantive contents of law. Human law is regulated, both in content and procedure, by practical reason. Practical reason, in Aquinas's view, is teleological and goal-oriented, in the sense that it is directed toward an end, which in this case is *the good*. According to him, "the first principle in the practical reason is one founded on the nature of good, viz., that *good is that which all things seek after*. Hence this is the first precept of law, that *good is to be done and promoted, and evil is to be avoided*."[35] Human law in Aquinas's

---

[35] Ibid., question 94, 2nd article, p. 774.

view, is a set of means (procedures, power, and criteria) for achieving the end of the good, in particular, the common good of a community. The notion of the good or common good specifies what is to be done or avoid-ed, and how best to train or discipline people, via the law and its coercive power of punishment, to do good and avoid evil in order to lead a life of virtue and in peace. Aquinas indicates that "in order that man might have peace and virtue, it was necessary for laws to be framed."[36] This is the pri-mary function of law. According to this descriptive, functional, and pro-cedural view, law must be sensitive to people's circumstances.

For Aquinas, "the natural law contains certain universal precepts which are everlasting; whereas human law contains certain particular pre-cepts, according to various circumstances."[37] In this sense, human laws must be understood in terms of procedures and substantive contents, which are relative to time, culture, and place. This is bolstered by his view that "laws imposed on men should also be in keeping with their con-dition, ... law should be possible both according to nature, and according to the customs of the country."[38] Human laws exist based on natural law and the descriptive procedural factors, which are contingent facts about human society, government, customs, and the peculiar circumstances of a country. He indicates that "custom has the force of law, abolishes law, and is the interpreter of law."[39] The contingent requirements of human soci-ety are important for understanding his descriptive procedural account of law, legal validity, legal obligation. The need for laws, which are essen-tial to a human society, is motivated by the fact that human beings have a natural inclination to live harmoniously with others in society. Human laws and the goal of common good are contingent reflections of different societies and the inclination of humans to live in society. Natural law pre-cepts represent the universal necessity for humans to live a socially good life of virtue. This universal inclination motivates people to seek via rea-son, human knowledge, and understanding, the best means including laws to lead a good life in a specific society.

36 Ibid., question 95, 1st article, p. 783.

37 Ibid., question 97, 1st article, p. 801.

38 Ibid., question 96, 2nd article, p. 792.

39 Ibid., question 97, 3rd article, p. 803.

People seek the best means relative to their situation by adopting and adapting rational procedures and moral contents that will help them to achieve their requisite goals of common good. Aquinas insists that laws must be framed by humans in the context of a given society as a means for achieving the requisite human ends of training people–via prohibitions—to act in a desirable way that is conducive to the common good of the society. The substantive content of a law is contingent because it is directed at the common good of a specific society. A law also has the feature of being a universal proposition because it derives from practical reason, which represents a universal nature of human beings and the universal human good that humans naturally seek. In Aquinas's view, "Such universal propositions of the practical reason that are directed to operations have the nature of law."[40] By 'operations' here in the context of practical reason, he means certain social and political structures, institutions, and procedures for doing what will achieve the desired ends or goals. Aquinas indicates that the nature of the end or operations to which a law is directed will determine the procedures and content of the law. Hence he argues that "there are various human laws according to the various forms of government."[41] The different forms of governments that are dictated by cultures and situations are different kinds of practical 'operations'. This suggests that laws, as the requisite means in the context of practical reason, are relative to or relationally framed to suit different operations, circumstances, structures, and ends.

AQUINAS'S VIEW OF LAW IN THE CONTEXT OF CURRENT DEBATES

We may better understand what he means by 'operations' as the procedures for working within a structure or institution, by paying attention to his example regarding the process of building a house. He suggests that there is a universal principle in the idea of law as a set of procedures and processes for working in a structure. Such a principle, as an element of practical reason, allows the universal idea or nature of law to be applicable to similar structures. In addition to indicating the universal and con-

[40] Ibid., question 90, 1st article, p. 743.
[41] Ibid., question 95, 4th article, p. 788.

tingent natures of law, it is pertinent to also understand that Aquinas was trying to do a number of related things in his account of law. One such thing was to give an account of the different senses in which the concept of law may be used. He sought to account for the core or paradigm sense of the concept of law, as distinguished from its perverted or peripheral sense. His account of natural law tries to capture the core or paradigm sense of law, as oppose to the perverted or peripheral sense of law. We must juxtapose the two senses of law on Aquinas's central point that there are two different *natures* or *essences* of law. Thus, a law must have an essential 'substantive content nature' as well as a 'descriptive procedural nature', which, in the 'core sense', must be morally good and just.

A law may be unjust in substantive content and still be a law in the 'peripheral sense' because it satisfies the descriptive 'proper' procedures of the state. Aquinas indicates these points as follows:

> A tyrannical law, through not being according to reason, is not a law, absolutely speaking, but rather a perversion of law; and yet in so far as it is something in *the nature of a law*, its aim is that the citizens be good. For it has *the nature of law* only in so far as it is an ordinance made by a superior to his subjects, and aims at being obeyed by them; and this is to make them good, not absolutely, but with respect to the particular government.[42]

The significant point from this passage is that a perverted tyrannical law is not a law in the absolute or core sense because it lacks a normative essence, which involves a morally good content and morally good procedures. As such, a tyrannical law is a law in the peripheral sense, in the sense of satisfying some criteria of legal validity, which means it has only a descriptive procedural *nature of a law*. This nature is contingent because it is relative to the descriptive features about the procedures and the good sought by a particular government. These features include the fact that (i) it is made by a country's superior, (ii) it is promulgated according to the country's criteria, (iii) it is meant to be obeyed by people within a territorial boundary, and (iv) it is backed by coercive force or punishment that is specified by a legitimate authority in the country. Aquinas insists that in its 'core' sense, the descriptive procedural nature

[42] Ibid., question 92, 1st article, p. 760.

of law must be normatively just. A law may have a just descriptive 'procedural nature' without having a just 'substantive content nature' and vice versa. A human law need not be procedurally and substantively just in order to be a law in a peripheral sense. Hence, a tyrannical law is a law in a perverted sense.

For Aquinas, an unjust law is a law, simply because it is appropriately promulgated and backed by force, albeit, in a perverted sense of law. Such a law exists as a law, only in a descriptive procedural sense of a law. Hence, in his view, human law, i.e., "Laws framed by man are either just or unjust."[43] In his view, a law may be immoral or unjust in different senses.[44] A law may be just or unjust in a substantive content sense, or a normative procedural sense, or a descriptive procedural sense. A law is unjust in a normative procedural sense if the processes of framing, promulgating, and applying a law in a legal system are unjust. A law is unjust in a descriptive procedural sense, if it fails to satisfy some community's criteria for identifying a law or if it does not follow the socially accepted process for making and promulgating a law. Such procedures may or may not be just. If a community's procedures are unjust, then a law that derives from them will be a law only in a perverted sense. A law that is unjust procedurally may, in its aim or application, be just, moral, and for the common good. Moreover, a law may be just in normative and descriptive procedural senses, but unjust in a substantive content sense. Being just in a descriptive procedural sense requires the proper exercise of power and authority by the person who has care of the community or has the responsibility to make law. Descriptive procedural justice simply requires that one follow the proper procedures for making law—which may or may not be normatively just—in virtue of which, a law is deemed legally valid in that society. Because of human fallibility in the use of reason, the fact that a law is just procedurally (i.e, descriptively or normatively) does not imply that it will be just in its substantive content or end, and vice versa.

The idea of practical reason, in terms of the best means or procedures, requires that we provide adequate strictures to prevent the lawgiver from

43 Ibid., question 96, 4th article, p. 795.

44 Ibid., question 96, 4th article, pp. 794-5 (emphasis on 'the nature of law' is mine).

misusing his power. The proper exercise of power requires that a law-giver make laws that have substantively good moral content. We may determine the extent to which the substantive content or end of a law is just based on its ability to satisfy the public interest, with respect to peo-ple's abilities to live a good life. Another sense of formal or procedural justice involves equal treatment of people or the imposition of equal bur-dens. Aquinas indicates that there is a sense of injustice "in respect of *the form*, as when burdens are imposed unequally on the community."[45] A violation of the elements and strictures or justice, such as the improper exercise of power or unequal application of law or unequal sharing or burden, constitutes one sense in which, according to Aquinas, a law may be unjust. Such a violation, which involves a formal sense of injustice does not necessarily imply that a law is unjust in substantive content. For instance, a judge may unequally place burdens or apply the law, and a lawgiver may abuse his power of framing laws, but such judgment or law may, in content, be substantively just, in the sense of prescribing a good conduct that serves the common good. A benevolent tyrant may unequal-ly impose burdens such as taxes on the poor and rich for the common good by using the money properly to help everyone lead a good life. In spite of the fact such a law is for the common good and moral in content, it is reasonable to say that it is unjust in a formal sense, simply because the unequal imposition of burdens people and the improper exercise of his power violate *the form* as opposed to the substantive content of jus-tice.[46]

Because human laws may not necessarily be just in content, it follows that an unjust law may be a law in some perverted descriptive procedur-al sense. For Aquinas, "every human law has just *so much of the nature of law* as it is derived from the law of nature. But if in any point it departs from the law of nature, it is no longer a law but a perversion of law."[47] The idea of having "so much of the nature of law" indicates that a human law may have different degrees or gradations of the core sense of the

[45] Ibid., question 96, 4th article, p. 795 (emphasis on 'the form' is mine; here Aquinas appears to be alluding to the formal sense of equality and justice).

[46] Ibid., question 96, 4th article, p. 795.

[47] Ibid., question 95, 2nd article, p. 784. (emphasis on 'so much of the nature of law' is mine).

nature of law, which is represented by natural law. In his view, the 'full', 'complete', or 'ideal' nature' of law, which is represented by natural law, must be understood in terms of the conjunction of the moral adequacy of each of the two natures of law. To have a moral 'procedural nature' without the moral 'content nature' is for a law *not* to have 'as much nature' as Aquinas would want, according to his core sense. This is because the law is not, in content, derived from the moral precepts of practical reason that represent natural law. This means that the law is unjust in one sense, which involves a substantive failure to achieve the requisite end of common good or match the precepts of natural law. The content aspect of human law seeks to specify people's rights, privileges, obligations, and immunities, and the nature of actions that are proscribed or permissible.

So, if we fail to fully appreciate Aquinas's substantive content and procedural *natures of law*, and the core and peripheral *senses of law*, then we cannot properly understand his account of law. The procedural and content natures of law are regulated by reason. Reason helps citizens and the lawgiver to appreciate the substantive moral content of a law, the proper exercise of law-making powers, and the proper processes and criteria for making laws. Aquinas's idea that 'an unjust law is not a law' must be understood as implying that an unjust law is not a law only in the core sense, in that it lacks moral procedures or substantive moral content. As such, it is not a reasonable *means* for achieving the morally good *end* of the common good. Thus, it falls short of the core sense of law or eternal law that natural law should aid human law to approximate or mirror.

In addition to his distinction between the peripheral and core senses of law, and the two different natures of law, Aquinas also sought to provide a typology of law. He indicates that there are four types of law: eternal, divine, natural, and human (positive) laws. These different types of law are connected but are also conceptually distinct. But Michael Baur suggests that there is a fifth type of law in Aquinas's typology, i.e., positive law, which "refers simply to any legislative enactment as it is factually given and enforceable through the power of the state, regardless of whether legislative enactment is good or not."[48] He argues that what distinguishes *positive law* from *human law* is that human law, in Aquinas's

48 Michael Baur, op. cit., p. 56.

normative view, cannot be said to be bad or unjust, whereas a positive can be said to be good or bad. In Baur's view, positive law is not, for Aquinas, necessarily a law because it lacks an adequate moral content, and as such, it does not have the normative nature or essence of law in the core sense.

I disagree with Baur's view that Aquinas did make such a distinction between *positive* and *human* law because there is no clear textual evidence.[49] Baur's characterization of human law, as distinct from positive law, is inconsistent with Aquinas's view that human law, i.e., "Laws framed by man are either just or unjust."[50] But I agree that Baur's distinction has a heuristic analytical value, in terms of how to properly understand Aquinas's account of the different *natures* and *senses* of law. This distinction does bolster my interpretation of Aquinas's theory. Positive law, in Baur's sense, captures the descriptive procedural nature of law. The core sense of human law, which a positive law would be a part of, only if it is morally adequate and just, does capture the normative nature of a law. A positive law, which is unjust in procedures or substantive content would be a perverted human law. Hence, Aquinas indicates that human law or positive law–which are synonymous—could be just or unjust. If positive or human law is good both in content and procedures, then it represents the core sense of law, but if it is bad in content or procedures, then it is not law in the core sense but only in a perverted sense.

John Finnis articulates the sense in which Aquinas's statement that, 'an unjust law is not a law' makes sense, since its literal understanding makes no sense. It makes sense in the context of his distinction among the substantive content, normative procedural, and descriptive procedural natures of law, and the core and peripheral senses of law. Aquinas's point is that if a law has a descriptive procedural nature without the moral pro-

---

[49] I disagree with Baur because Aquinas seems to use positive law and human law interchangeably, and he sometimes talks about positive human law and refers to them as "laws framed by man." It is not true that human law could not be bad because Aquinas does indicate that human law could be just or unjust. In other words, Baur is wrong in thinking that a law must necessarily be good in order to be human law in a descriptive sense. Aquinas talks about positive law or positive human law in question 95, fourth article, pp. 787-788. Here, he discusses the appropriateness of the division of human law or positive human law and indicates that positive law may be divided into law of nations and civil law.

[50] *Summa Theologica*, op. cit., question 96, 4th article, p. 795.

cedures and substantive moral content, which means that it is unjust or immoral, then it is a perverted sense of law. In Finnis's view,

> Aquinas carefully avoids saying flatly that 'an unjust law is not a law: *lex injusta non est lex*'. But in the end it would have mattered little had he said just that. For the statement either is pure nonsense, flatly self-contradictory, or else is a dramatization of the point more literally made by Aquinas when he says that an unjust law is not a law in the focal sense of the term 'law' [i.e., *simpliciter*] notwithstanding that it is law in a secondary sense of that term [i.e., secundum quid].[51]

I agree with Finnis's point above that, the sense in which Aquinas says that an unjust law is not a law, is similar to the sense in which he also denies that 'an unjust judgment of a court is not a judgment'. Aquinas would accept that such an unjust judgment is perverted but still a legal judgment anyway in a purely descriptive procedural sense: that is, it describes *the fact* that the judge is merely following the community's procedures in carrying out his legal duty. Following such procedures does not make any normative judgment regarding whether or not such a duty or judgment is just or moral.

A judgment is legal in the core sense only if the legal procedures are just and the substantive content of the judgment that derives from such procedures is also just. This means that a legal judgment has the two natures of law. If the substantive content and procedural natures of law are moral, then the judgment is valid in the core sense of a law. I disagree with Finnis's view that it would have mattered a little had Aquinas said flatly that an unjust law is not a law. My disagreement is underscored by Finnis's own indication that there is a shift in Aquinas's language, which indicates the different natures and senses of law. This use of language involves "a supple subordination of words to a shifting focus of interest" in the core sense of law, as opposed to a self contradiction.[52] The lack of flat denial, that an unjust law is not law, is significant. This significance can be captured if we understand the denial in the context of Aquinas's accounts of the typology of law, different natures of human law, and the

---

[51] John Finnis, op. cit., p. 364.

[52] Ibid., p. 364, note 13.

core and peripheral senses of the concept of law. Such accounts explain and justify Aquinas's view that if a law does not have the requisite normative natures in the *core sense* of having both *moral procedures and substantive moral content*, this does not mean that it does not have the nature of a law in the peripheral sense or in the descriptive procedural sense of *being promulgated, being backed by force, and thus, having a binding force*.

John Finnis has captured Aquinas's central points regarding the normative ideas of legal validity and essence of law, and the *core sense* of the concept of law by translating these ideas into contemporary legal concepts in order to place them in the context of modern jurisprudential debates. According to him,

> If we may translate the relevant portion of, for example, Thomas Aquinas's theory into Kelsenian terminology (as far as possible), it runs as follows: The legal validity (in the focal, moral sense of 'legal validity') of positive law is derived from its rational connection with (i.e. derivation from) natural law, and this connection holds good, normally, if and only if (i) the law originates in a way which is legally valid (in the specially restricted purely legal sense of 'legal validity') and (ii) the law is not materially unjust either in its content or in relevant circumstances of its positing. Aquinas's discussion of these points is under-elaborated, in relation to the modern jurisprudential debate.[53]

Finnis is correct to point out that these central points in Aquinas's theory are under-elaborated, and I dare to say, his contributions to modern jurisprudential debates are unappreciated. This is partly because his view has been narrowly and mistakenly construed. For Aquinas, the moral validity or core sense of law, which is one nature of law and one sense of 'legal validity', derives from its rational derivation from eternal law via natural law. It appears that Aquinas's endorsement of St. Augustine's statement that, 'a law that is not just seems to be no law at all' has not been properly understood because it has not been placed in the proper context of his account of the different natures and senses of law.

[53] Ibid., p. 27.

CONCLUSION

Aquinas's account of law cannot be understood solely in terms of the universal precepts of natural law that constrain the substantively just and morally good content and procedures of human law. And his view of law must not be seen solely and purely as normative, divorced from the contingent, human, rational, societal, and descriptive procedural elements of law. Procedurally, being a human law indicates that it has gone through the processes or satisfied the criteria for determining how laws are made, promulgated, and administered, and that it is made within the limits and scope of the power of those in authority. The core sense and substantive content nature of human law require that a promulgated law must be just and consistent with natural law. However, if a human law is inconsistent with natural law or is bad, it is nonetheless a valid positive human law, except that it is a perverted human law. Aquinas did emphasize in his typology of law the conceptual distinction between natural law and human law, and between legal and moral obligation. He did not conflate them as some critics charge.

AQUINAS' ECONOMIC ETHICS: "PROFOUNDLY ANTICAPITALISTIC?"

Stephen Rowntree, S.J.

INTRODUCTION

After the actually existing socialist economies of Eastern Europe and the Soviet Union collapsed in 1989, capitalism claimed a clear and undisputed victory in the decades-long conflict between the two systems. But what is and what ought to be need not be the same. Capitalism could everywhere be triumphant and nonetheless be morally defective. To get some perspective on the moral status of capitalism, I propose once again to look at Aquinas' economic ethics.

One might object to this project as highly anachronistic: Aquinas had nothing to say about capitalism, one way or the other. It did not exist when he wrote. As evidence one might cite the *Communist Manifesto*. Marx and Engels interpret commercial capitalism as a creation of the post-1492 voyages of exploration. On the other hand, historians of medieval economics have shown that extensive manufacturing, commerce, and long-distance trade flourished in a number of industries in the 12th and 13th centuries.[1] Aquinas could have observed capitalism. What did he think of it, if anything?

Eleonore Stump in her recent overview of Aquinas' philosophy concludes that his view of economics is "profoundly anticapitalistic."[2] While Stump doesn't explicitly define what she means by capitalism, a quick look at how this term is understood in economics will help to appreciate Aquinas' moral assessment of capitalism.

The term capitalism comes from "capital." A popular introductory text observes that capital is one of the factors of production (the other two are land and labor). Capital refers to economic resources that are used to produce other goods. For example, machines that make auto parts. In the case of trade, capital would be the ships, crews' wages, and money to buy

---

[1] See, for example, Robert Lopez, *The Commercial Revolution of the Middle Ages: 950-1350* (Englewood Cliffs, NJ: Prentice-Hall, 1971), 130-47; *The Birth of Europe* (New York: M. Evans, 1966), 278-307.

[2] Eleanore Stump, *Aquinas* (London and New York: Routledge, 2003), 337.

products in one place to sell for profit in another. The essential note of capitalism lies in the private ownership of capital, and therefore its owners' claims to any profits made.[3] A second note of capitalism as a form of economic organization consists of markets with prices established by free bargaining between buyers and sellers as basic ordering principle.[4]

Pope John Paul II's 1991 encyclical, *Centesimus Annus* understood capitalism to be an "economic system which recognizes the fundamental and positive role of business: the market, private property, and the resulting responsibility for the means of production," but goes on to note "it would perhaps be more appropriate to speak of a 'business economy,' 'market economy,' or simply 'free economy.'"[5]

The most fundamental objection to capitalism lies not in the mechanism of prices and markets to organize production and distribution (though Marx himself did object to them and imagined their being replaced by planning), but in the ownership of capital, especially the right to profits earned by capital. Marx held that labor is the source of all economic value, including what is earned by capital. This is so because capital goods that produce additional economic value are themselves products of labor. Marx's *Capital* tells the story of how workers were deprived of their land and tools, and hence had only their labor to sell to those who had dispossessed them.[6] The revolution that overthrows and dispossesses the capitalists will return ownership of the means of pro-

[3] Paul Samuelson and William Nordhaus, *Economics*, 15th ed. (New York: McGraw-Hill, 1994), 8, 29-30.

[4] Economists classify economic systems in terms of three pure forms that may be (and are) mixed together in varying combinations. An economic system determines what and how much is produced, how it is produced, and who gets what. The pure forms are (1) tradition: what has always been done in the past guides current choices; (2) planning: some one (or group) decides before hand the answers to these questions and designs a comprehensive plan to achieve them; (3) markets: individuals are granted property rights in the factors of production and freedom to choose occupations, and decide what's best for themselves guided by price signals. The market system with no central direction, coordinates billions of individual decisions, the results of which are definite kinds and amounts of goods and services, produced in particular ways, and distributed in varying proportions to individuals and families. Samuelson and Nordhaus, 5-6.

[5] Pope John Paul II, *Centesimus Annus* (Vatican City, 1991), #42.

[6] Karl Marx, *Capital*, vol. 1, Part 8, "So-Called Primitive Accumulation."

duction to the collective ownership of workers. Capitalist profits will disappear, though saving from current production for investment in new capital goods will continue to be necessary. Workers, however, will be the exclusive beneficiaries of the surplus created. Such is the most profound and fundamental form of anticapitalism.

R.H. Tawney, the English Christian socialist and sociologist, believed that Aquinas held the labor theory of value. Thus he made the striking claim that "the last of the Schoolmen was Karl Marx."[7] Understanding how and why Tawney is mistaken about Aquinas will be essential to understanding Aquinas' attitude toward capitalism.

While the labor theory of value implies a radical criticism of capitalism's essential feature of capitalist profit, this theory is not Stump's reason for believing Aquinas to be profoundly anticapitalistic. Let us then examine her understanding of Aquinas as a first step to determining his economic ethics.

Stump defends her claim that Aquinas opposes capitalism first by observing that injustice results when one person desires to have more good things (material possessions, honors) than another and fewer evil things.[8] She quotes him further that "justice implies equality of a certain sort."[9] I suspect that the link between justice and equality refers much more to a formal equality than Stump realizes. Aquinas surely holds with Aristotle that justice involves treating equals equally and unequals unequally,[10] and so one cannot conclude that he holds for substantive economic equality and opposes capitalism because it generates economic inequalities (which admittedly it does).[11]

Of greatest interest for understanding Aquinas' economic views are *Summa Theologiae* II-II, Questions 77 and 78 where he treats explicitly

---

[7] R.H. Tawney, *Religion and the Rise of Capitalism* (Gloucester, MA: Peter Smith, 1962), 36.

[8] Stump, 318, quoting *Summa Theologiae* II-II, 59, 1.

[9] Stump, 318, quoting *Summa Theologiae* II-II, 57, 1.

[10] Aristotle, *Politics*, III, 9, 1280a7.

[11] Aquinas makes this point in commenting on the *Nichomachean Ethics'* Book 5, chap. 3 discussion of justice as a "proportional mean." *Commentary on the Nichomachean Ethics*, trans. By C.I. Litzinger, vol. 1 (Chicago: Henry Regnery, 1964), 402.

of buying and selling (q. 77) and usury (q. 78). Stump makes several points relevant to her interpretation of Aquinas' anticapitalism in discussing these questions. She notes that he has exigent standards for a commutatively just exchange. Since the criterion on commutative justice is strict equality, an exchange in which one party benefits while the other party loses is unjust.[12] A just price in an exchange is not simply one that the parties agree to, but it has an objective measure intrinsic to that which is exchanged: "Aquinas thinks there is a just price for a thing, which is measured not by the demand for that thing but rather by the thing's own worth."[13] She confesses she doesn't understand how apart from desire or need one assesses the worth of something bought or sold. But she takes this to be clear from the words of *Summa Theologiae* II-II, 77, 1: "To sell for more or to buy for less than a thing is worth, is, therefore, unjust and illicit in itself." Understanding Aquinas' view of a just price as a price intrinsic to an object very much counts against the markets characteristic of capitalism. For market prices of a good vary as conditions of supply and demand change, rising when demand rises, falling when demand falls, falling when supply increases and rising when supply falls. All the while the intrinsic value of the good remains the same.

Stump points out further that Aquinas explicitly rules out great need as a reason for raising the price to a buyer. He explains that in such cases the extra worth is due to the buyer's situation and therefore the seller would be charging extra for something that is not her own.[14] But if selling something for what it is objectively worth causes the seller a loss, she may sell it for more, but for no more extra than the extra worth it had for her. For in this case the source of extra value is the seller's. Hence the seller can charge extra to make up for her own loss. Again, such contingencies, one of which does justify a price increase, the other of which doesn't, are not taken account of in ordinary market exchanges.

Stump finds relevant to her argument that in ruling out fraud (which in some form almost all defenders of markets also rule out), Aquinas also insists that the seller must compensate for defects unrecognized at the

---

12 Stump, 318.

13 Stump, 318.

14 For this see *Summa Theologiae* II-II, 67, 1.

time of sale, but discovered later. And likewise if a seller mistakenly sells a higher value object thinking it of lesser value, for example, mistaking a solid gold object for a gold-plated one, the buyer who discovers the mistake must pay extra (or return the object). Stump takes such a strict view of just trading to rule out what she calls "economic luck."[15]

I suspect that most people today would consider making compensation in these cases at best a matter of counsel or supererogation, and not at all a matter of strict justice. Current law certainly would not require lucky buyers to reject their good fortune. The case of defects discovered later may be a different matter, especially if the product has a warranty that is in effect.

Aquinas's rejection of taking interest on loans most obviously justifies Stump's view that he is firmly against capitalism. For capitalism without banks, lending, and credit controlled by individuals, partnerships, and companies—that is, capitalism without capitalists—is impossible. Stump herself interprets one of his arguments against usury to be that it leads to some becoming richer (lenders), others poorer (borrowers). She quotes *Summa Theologiae* II-II, 78, 1: "it is manifest that this leads to inequality which is contrary to justice."[16]

While lending money expecting something in addition to the sum lent (interest) stands clearly forbidden, Stump thinks Aquinas also finds earning a profit by buying goods for one price and selling them for a higher one to be morally questionable. She quotes *Summa Theologiae* II-II, q 77, 4, 2 to support her case: "It is…contrary to justice to sell something for more than it is worth or to buy it for less. But a commercial trader who does business by selling something for more than he himself paid must have either bought it for less than it is worth or be selling it for more."[17] Stump acknowledges that Aquinas answers this weighty objection by asserting that seeking to make a profit by trading is not in itself wrong. Modest profit earned to provide for one's family is permissible. Stump interprets this reply to be a narrow exception to the general rule that trading for profit is wrong because inherently motivated by greed.

---

[15] Stump, 319.

[16] Stump, 319.

[17] Fuller quotation from Blackfriars ed. than her condensation.

The merchant's permissible profit is not actually profit, but a return for the labor of trading: "...he still thinks that trading for profit has something base about it since it serves the lust for money. Nonetheless, Aquinas explains, by trading, a man might seek only modest profit for the upkeep of his household. In that case he is not seeking profit itself, but only an appropriate reward for his labor in the business of trading."[18]

Stump finds several additional arguments beyond the prohibition of taking interest on a loan and limits on profits from trading for Aquinas' criticism of capitalism, but these are not relevant for the purposes of this paper.

But does Stump get Aquinas right? Is Aquinas "profoundly anticapitalistic?" I will try to show that a close reading of the two essential texts: *Summa Theologiae* II-II, 77 and 78, and of the secondary interpretations (most of older vintage), leads to a different conclusion about Aquinas' view of the essential features of capitalism (product/labor markets, financial markets). Aquinas' views on economics have been much investigated (and much disputed). My paper will try to bring together to this time and place widely dispersed interpretations of Aquinas on these points. The most helpful older secondary sources are John T. Noonan, *The Scholastic Analysis of Usury*,[19] John W. Baldwin, *Medieval Theories of the Just Price: Romanists, Canonists, and Theologians in the Twelfth and Thirteenth Centuries*,[20] and Raymond de Roover's assorted papers on scholastic economics.[21] The recent study of Odd Langholm, *The Legacy of Scholasticism in Economic Thought* confirms the conclusions of these older sources about Aquinas and the overall development of medieval and early modern scholastic economic ethics.[22]

---

[18] Stump, 320.

[19] Cambridge, MA: Harvard University Press, 1957.

[20] Philadelphia: The American Philosophical Society, 1959.

[21] "The Concept of the Just Price: Theory and Economic Policy," *Journal of Economic History* 18, no. 4 (1958): 418-34; "Scholastic Economics: Survival and Lasting Influence from the Sixteenth Century to Adam Smith," in Jules Kirsher, ed., *Business, Banking, and Economic Thought* (Chicago: University of Chicago Press, 1974), 306-335

[22] Cambridge: Cambridge University Press, 1998.

My thesis is, first, Aquinas finds nothing intrinsically wrong in either a merchant's buying and selling for profit, nor, second, in any one's investing capital for profit by financing such trade. Third, such activities must be conducted in accord with strict justice (which he defines clearly), however permissive the law may be about sharp dealing which exploits the need, gullibility, or ignorance of either buyer or seller. The justice demanded is not a counsel of perfection, but a mandatory precept requiring strict restitution of unjustly acquired gains. Aquinas thus shows how markets for goods/services, and markets for finance—the two basic elements of capitalism—are morally permissible if carried out in accord with strict justice.

One might understand this view of capitalism to confirm Stump's basic judgment that he is "profoundly anticapitalistic," in the sense that all existing capitalisms fail to meet his strict standards. Be that as it may, I shall try to show that Aquinas does define an ethics—a business ethics, if you will—that would make a moral capitalism possible.

AQUINAS ON BUYING AND SELLING FOR PROFIT

At first hearing *Summa Theologiae* II-II, 77, 1 and 4 soundparadoxical, even contradictory. The answer to the question in article 1, "is one entitled to sell something for more that it is worth" is a clear no. On the other hand, the answer to the question in article 4, "is one entitled to make profits by selling something for more than one had paid for it" is yes (though within limits, as Stump noted).

The first objection to the view that one is not entitled to sell something for more than it is worth appeals to law ("the Code" of Justinian). This law allows buyers and sellers to deceive one another about the value of goods. This law derives from the Roman law of sale. Baldwin gives the relevant background. He characterizes Roman law's view of buying and selling as "laissez-faire." Thus Ulpian (3rd cent. CE) quotes Pomponius (late 2nd cent. BCE): "Pomponius says it is naturally permitted to parties to circumvent each other in the price of buying and selling." Another 3rd century jurist (Paul) elaborated on Pomponius: "In buying and selling natural law permits the one party to buy for less and the other part to sell for more than the thing is worth, thus each party is allowed to outwit the other."[23] What matters legally was the price the parties agreed to. The language of "naturally" and "natural law" suggest Ulpian and Paul judged the agreement of the parties was also the last word morally, not just legally. Such a view is echoed by libertarians today: for them, as for Ulpian and Paul, what makes an exchange morally just is the agreement of the wills of buyer and seller, that and nothing more. And why not? Both parties must have been satisfied with the result or they would not have agreed.

Aquinas rejects the view that the freely bargained price is necessarily just, and thereby rejects the law's permission as the measure of justice. The law may allow what is unjust and hence legal permissibility does not guarantee moral permissibility.

Roman law itself imposed certain limits on bargains. Courts could order restitution in cases of fraud and when land was sold for a price that was 50% greater or less than the just price (so-called "*laesio enormis*").[24]

However permissive human law might be in these matters, God's law is different: "nothing contrary to virtue" goes "unpunished." And one who has taken advantage of the other to negotiate an unjust price must make restitution ("providing the loss is an important one").[25]

Both the Roman law of *laesio* and the divine law of just price presume some measure of price that can be different from a negotiated price. Libertarians, who accept mutual agreement, absent force or fraud, as the measure of a just bargain find this notion of a measure of objective price extremely perplexing, not to say utterly confused.

Three possibilities have been suggested about what an objective price might mean. The first refers to classical metaphysics' concept of degrees of being or reality. Thus a rock as an inanimate object has less being than a plant, which is living. Among living things, insects have more being than plants, and animals more than insects. The human animal's spiritual aspect puts humans at the summit of animals. But pure spirits, such as angels, have even more being than humans. The highest place in the hier-

[23] See Baldwin, 16-20. The quotes are from 17.

[24] For specific provisions concerning *laesio*, see Baldwin, 18.

[25] *Summa Theologiae* II-II, 77, 1, 1. Aquinas notes that determining the just price exactly may be difficult. Parties must do the best they can: "with the result that giving or taking a little here or there does not upset the balance of justice."

archy of being is God—Being Itself—who therefore transcends all lesser beings. Aquinas, following Augustine, explicitly rejects this possible understanding of objective value. For buying and selling concern things useful for meeting human needs. A mosquito may have more intrinsic being than a nail, but if my shoe heel is loose, I need a nail. Thus Aquinas observes:

> It is Augustine who points out that the price of commercial commodities ("rerum venalium") is not assessed in accordance with their relative position on some absolute scale in the natural world, for a horse is sometimes sold for more than a slave [!!], but in accord with their usefulness to men.[26]

A second possibility, a once common interpretation, took the cost of production to constitute a product's just price. A just price was thus the sum of the cost of the materials, labor, and capital that went into making it. This view also provided a measure for a just wage, for the just price of the labor that made a product was a wage sufficient to provide a decent standard of living for the worker and his family.[27]

Of course, costs of production in this sense would vary from place to place, and one time to another, but the cost of production for any given product would be a definite amount, and in that sense, objective. That free bargaining would settle on that precise amount was quite unlikely. On this account the freely agreed price was not a just price.

This view of just price implies tight control and regulation of wages and prices. Every worker must earn, at a minimum, a wage sufficient to support a decent standard of living, and prices of products and services must be high enough to cover such a minimum wage for all workers.[28] Such a view of just price (including wages) certainly implies that wages and prices produced by the vagaries of supply and demand in response to price signals, i.e. by markets, will be one thing and just wages and prices

[26] *Summa Theologiae* II-II, 77, 2, 3. Aquinas' reference to Augustine is to *City of God*, Book XI, chap. 16.

[27] See Langholm, chap. 7, "Wages and Labor," 118-136, and de Roover, "Just Price:" 418-21.

[28] See John A. Ryan's *A Living Wage*, (New York: Macmillan, 1912) for one influential discussion of what would laws and policies would be required to guarantee a living wage.

quite another. If this were Aquinas' understanding, he would indeed oppose one of the essentials features of capitalism as defined above.

The third possible way to understand just prices acknowledges that prices established in markets with many buyers and sellers (i.e. absent monopoly or monopsony) are just prices. Prices established in such open/free markets do represent the vagaries of supply and demand. If people start to eat less beef, beef prices will fall, no matter how much it cost cattlemen and meat packers to produce sirloin steaks. They may well suffer losses. On the other hand, if beef consumption goes up, the profits of cattlemen and packers may increase as prices rise. Prices therefore rise and fall. How can they be in any sense objective? Doesn't this mean the freely bargained price is the just price? Not necessarily.

The relevant price objectivity for establishing a just price lies in the market price set by the interaction of many buyers and sellers (the more the better, in fact). Thus for example, the stock market reports show the closing prices of all the shares traded that day on an exchange. The closing price is where the price settled after all trades of that stock that day. This price is the combined result of all the particular decisions of all the buyers and sellers. Most sellers at a particular price sold believing or guessing or anticipating the price would go lower. Buyers bought in hope of a higher price. Each sale or buy was determined by such conflicting expectations (that is, "subjectively," in this limited sense). But the overall outcome is a set closing price.

The moral significance of the market price as the just price lies in the difference between the outcome of many acts of buying and selling, and the outcome of a particular sale. Thus I think we should understand Aquinas' first question about selling something for "more than it is worth," to refer to selling something for more than the current market price. Where markets are well established and prices fully and rapidly communicated, a knowledgeable buyer would know this price, and would not pay more. But where markets were not well established, or prices not widely known, a buyer might take advantage to sell for more than the current market price. Aquinas' discussion implies that a seller (or buyer) has a positive duty to disclose to the other party the market price. Non-disclosure constitutes fraud. Thus we can understand his reply that to sell something for more that it is worth defrauds the one ignorant of the current price: "To practice fraud so as to sell something for more than its just price is an outright sin in so far as one is deceiving one's neighbor to his detriment."[29]

Aquinas recognizes that people who exchange do so for their mutual benefit (*pro communi utilitate utriusque*). Exchange is mutually beneficial "in so far as each one needs something the other party has" (quoting Aristotle, *Politics*, Book 1, chap. 9. 1257a6). Both Aristotle and Aquinas recognized the essentials of what "marginal analysis" formalized in the 19th century: imagine two persons, one with 20 loaves of bread and no wine, and the other with 5 bottles of wine and no bread. Each will gain by trading. For each needs some of what the other has in relative abundance. The essential mutual benefit of exchange is intuitively clear. Marginal analysis spells this out by saying the marginal benefit of the first bottle of wine for some one with 20 loaves of bread is greater than the marginal benefit of the 15th-20th loaves of bread that it costs, let us assume, for one bottle of wine. The converse is true for the person with 5 bottles of wine and no bread. As one commentator points out, we can think of each "profiting" from this trade, in that each is overall better off after this exchange than before.[30] This analysis does not presume that each person's marginal benefit from exchange is equal—only that each is better off after the exchange than before, i.e. absolutely better off, though one may have gained relatively more than the other.

The commutative (arithmetical) equality that characterizes a just exchange cannot lie in the benefits received. The equality lies in the seller charging the buyer the market price. Thus if the market price for the new Cambridge edition of Kant's *Critique of Pure Reason* is $29.95 and I pay the bookstore clerk $29.95 for the book, the exchange is arithmetically equal. I have exchanged $29.95 for a book worth $29.95. To put it simply, using Aristotle's distinction between "use" and "exchange" values, the different use values of the goods differ for the parties (hence the reason for the exchange), but what is exchanged is of equal monetary value, that is of equal exchange value ($29.95 for a book costing $29.95).

[29] *Summa Theologiae* II-II, 77, 1.

[30] James Child, "Profit: The Concept and Its Moral Features, *Social Philosophy and Policy*, 15 (2), 268-82.

This distinction explains why people exchange (each is better off than before it), but how such exchanges can also be equal. The different benefits gained have equal exchange values.

This analysis likewise solves the puzzle of how merchants can make a monetary profit, i.e. sell for more than they paid. It is unjust to sell at a particular time and place for more than the market price at that time and place. But to buy at the market price in one place and to transport the goods to another place where the market price is higher is commutatively just since the just price is paid in both places. Of course, this is precisely what merchants and traders do: buy goods in a place where they are relatively cheap because abundant to sell them in another place where they are relatively more expensive because scarce.

Aquinas follows Aristotle in pointing to the moral dangers of such trading: when people exchange to meet their needs, such exchange is limited because needs are limited. However, buying and selling for profit has no intrinsic limit. The potential for financial gain without limit makes avarice an occupational danger for merchants: "in itself [exchange for gain] feeds the acquisitive urge which knows no limits but tends to infinity."[31] He thinks, therefore, that trading for financial gain (*negotiatio*) is intrinsically dubious (*secundum se considerata, quandam turpitudinem habet*) because as such it does not fulfill good or necessary purposes (*inquantum non importat de sui ratione finem honestum vel necessarium*). Surprisingly, he goes on to claim that there is nothing intrinsic to profit seeking that is deficient or contrary to virtue. It is permissible if directed to good or necessary ends. It seems to me this is also true of trading when directed to good ends. I fail to see the grounds for holding trading to be intrinsically dubious while profit seeking is not.

In any case, the analysis of the logic of trade shows why and how merchants do provide benefits to buyers in the form of use values. Thus Aquinas writing about ways that profits can be justified notes that a trader promotes the public good by helping to assure adequate supplies of goods. The merchant's profit is the reward for the labor involved and not a pure windfall. He also notes that profits are morally justified when moderate and used by him to support his family or to help the poor.[32]

---

[31] *Summa Theologiae* II-II, 77, 4.

[32] Ibid.

Economists show that when markets are open profits tend to be moderate. For when markets are open, high profits attract competitors and high profits are competed away. But Aquinas is correct in his claim that the market itself does not assure moral or virtuous use of profits.

I am reading Aquinas to favor trade and exchange at market prices—even trade and exchange for profits. The tradition he inherited, especially from the Fathers of the Church, was much more critical of commerce. I think his effort to harmonize these sources with his own more positive view explains some anomalies. I have in mind especially the distinction he makes between non-merchants who, incidentally as it were, come to sell something for a higher price than they paid for it, and those whose occupation is to buy at one price and to sell at a higher. In describing what is permissible for the "accidental trader," Aquinas gives the fullest account of the several justifications for earning a profit. This person is permitted to ask for a price higher than the one he paid:

> either because he has improved the thing in some fashion, or because prices have gone up in response to local changes or the lapse of time, or because he has incurred risks in transporting it about or in having it delivered.[33]

Samuel Hollander reads this to mean that only the accidental trader is entitled to profit for the latter two reasons mentioned.[34] Such a reading would be consistent with the comment about the intrinsically dubious character of commerce, but would not be consistent with what is said about the reasons why limited profits are permitted for those whose business is trade. Read affirmatively, this passage expands on the reasons why traders' (accidental and professional) profits are justified. Furthermore, who but a professional trader could be described as assuming risks in transporting goods from one place to another?

Robert Lopez shows that in fact traders did provide important benefits to the largely rural communities of the 12th and 13th centuries. He grants that the development of trade in the 13th century took place at the heights of the economy, while rural life remained the same. But still

---

[33] *Summa Theologiae* II-II, 77, 4, 2.

[34] Samuel Hollander, "On the Interpretation of the Just Price," *Kyklos* 18, 4 (1965), 627.

peasants did benefit. Assuring adequate supplies of necessities was a
vital function of traders that saved communities from starvation in time
of famine. The good effects Aquinas mentions as justifications for commerce were sometimes vital to the survival of poor people:

> What benefits does the Commercial Revolution offer for the
> underprivileged peasant? One only, perhaps, but an important
> one: the almost complete disappearance of the specter of
> famine. Not only in affluent Italy and in fertile France and
> England, but also in the Low Countries and Germany, chroni-
> clers mention fewer than ten years of general famine during
> the 12th century, and two or three only in the 13th. This is due
> primarily to the peasants themselves, to their harvests; but also
> to the fact that when the harvest fails, grain may be obtained
> from distant countries. In 1276, for instance, the Commune of
> Genoa appeals to Manuel Zeccaria...to import grain from the
> Balkans as a matter of urgency, and is thereby enabled to 'open
> its hands in charity' and feed a host of refugees who have come
> from as far as France.[35]

Further evidence that the occupation of trading for profit can be
morally permissible is found in *Summa Theologiae* II-II, 77, 3. There
Thomas asks, "Is the seller bound to declare any defect in the thing sold?"
The answer, as we might expect, is a clear and emphatic yes. In the
course of making the point that a current flaw renders the current value
less than its value would be without the flaw, Aquinas distinguishes this
situation from a *future* loss of value. The situation he refers to is a case
Cicero discusses in *De Officiis*, III, 13. In Cicero's case, a grain dealer
brings a shipload of corn to a city suffering famine. The corn will, therefore, command a high price. Aquinas mentions the high price, but not the
reason for it. The question is whether the merchant, who knows that additional supplies are on the way, can sell at the current high price or must
reveal that other ships are soon to land. If he does, people may well wait
to buy (Aquinas, recall, does not mention famine) when prices have fall-
en because of the increased supply. Aquinas distinguishes between
revealing a current defect, justifying a lower price now, from revealing a
future event that will cause the market price to fall. His answer is perhaps somewhat surprising:

---

[35] Lopez, *The Birth of Europe*, 298.

A commodity with a flaw in it has a different value now than it would appear to have, whereas what is in question in the case put forward is a future loss of value because of the advent of dealers unknown to the buyers. It follows that a seller who sells something according to its market price would not seem to be acting unjustly if he fails to disclose a future contingency (unde venditor qui vendit rem secundum pretium quod invenit, non videtur contra iustitiam facere si quod futurum est non exponat).[36]

He acknowledges that to reveal that ships are coming or to lower the price would be more virtuous, but not required by justice.

Aquinas' answer is surprising because Cicero had given a different response to the case. According to Cicero, the dealer is obliged to disclose that ships are on the way. This disclosure is obligatory and not simply a matter of counsel or supererogation as it is for Aquinas.[37]

For those who interpret Aquinas to take for granted that current market prices are just prices (and hence approve markets), this passage is their proof text par excellence.[38] The conclusion that Aquinas approves market determination of prices (and hence this aspect of capitalism) follows from his view that just prices are prices established in open markets. Selling something for what it is worth means to sell it for its current market price. This is a demand of strict justice, though not of law. It is possible to make a just profit when selling if one has bought something at its current market place at one time and sells it later when the market price has risen. Economists call this "arbitrage." Its overall effect is to bring prices in different places closer together. In a world of instantaneous communication, prices everywhere would quickly become the same as traders quickly exhausted arbitrage opportunities. Aquinas's view of just transactions suggests a world of transparent, set prices known to buyers and sellers, but especially to sellers. They would sell to all buyers at the same (market) price whether the buyers were knowledgeable or ignorant. No opportunities for bargaining would exist except if a seller valued

36 *Summa Theologiae* II-II, 77, 3, 4.

37 *De Officiis*, Book III, xii, 56 (Loeb ed. 325).

38 See for example, Raymond de Roover, "The Concept of the Just Price: Theory and Economic Policy," 422.

something more than the market did. Such a seller could justly ask for a premium to compensate for this extra personal value. The seller could not justly ask for or accept a higher price than the market price even if the buyer were willing to pay it. For in that case, the seller would receive extra for what is not his own, but the buyer's, i.e. the readiness to pay more.[39] As Noonan reports, Scotus, for one disagreed with this latter conclusion. Why if an eager buyer was willing to pay a premium, knowing full well the market price (i.e. the just price), should the seller not be permitted to accept this freely and knowingly offered higher price?[40]

Aquinas states a very strict standard of fairness in buying and selling. A seller must not take advantage, for example, of a buyer's need or ignorance. Everyone must receive fair treatment. A mutually agreed price need not be the just price because the price a buyer is willing to pay ranges from the market price (below which we assume the seller will not sell) to a maximum (one's "reserve price") more than which a buyer is not willing to pay.[41]

Kant gives an example that helps to clarify the import of Aquinas' norm of just selling. Kant speaks of a shopkeeper's duty to charge every customer the same price: "For, example, it certainly conforms with duty that a shopkeeper not overcharge an inexperienced customer, and where there is a good deal of trade a prudent [Aquinas would say a just] merchant does not overcharge but keeps a fixed general price for everyone, so that a child can buy from him as well as everyone else."[42] Kant's comment presumes the same standard for just selling as Aquinas.'

---

[39] See *Summa Theologiae* II-II, 77, 1.

[40] Noonan, 86-87.

[41] I am especially indebted to Barbara Fried's *The Progressive Assault on Laissez Faire* (Cambridge, MA: Harvard University Press, 1998) for clarifying this point. Fried draws on Alan Wertheimer's suburb *Exploitation* (Princeton: Princeton University Press, 1996), 210-16.

[42] *Groundwork of the Metaphysics of Morals* (4:397), in *Practical Philosophy* (Cambridge Edition of the Works of Immanuel Kant) (Cambridge: Cambridge University Press, 1996), 53. Kant is concerned that the genuinely moral merchant does this *because* it is the just action. He implies that a prudent, but unjust merchant does this simply because customers who discovered they had been taken advantage of would not come back.

AQUINAS ON CAPITALIST INVESTMENT

Noonan reminds us that Aquinas' treatment of buying an selling for profit (just price) differs significantly from his treatment of lending at interest. The former is morally permissible under the conditions explained above. The latter is never permissible. So it might seem that the distinctive capitalist element of capitalism (investment for profit) is excluded. If true, this seems to justify the charge that Aquinas is profoundly anticapitalistic.

Lending and investment for profit are closely linked in a mature economy such as ours. Entrepreneurs borrow money from banks to start new businesses, investors to buy stocks and bonds, farmers to finance each year's new crop. Such borrowers put other people's savings to work to produce profits. The first charge on these profits pays the lenders for the use of savers' money. Lenders in turn first pay savers for the use of the savers' deposits.

The economic context for a ban on charging interest on a loan differed considerably from our own. People who could manage to save saved for a rainy day, not for investment. A person or family could be deprived of its means of living by crop failure or other natural disaster. In such a case, they might borrow money simply in order to survive until they could plant and harvest a new crop. To make any charge beyond the return of the money borrowed would be to take advantage of others' misfortunes. People who suffered such a disaster might well to agree to pay interest if this were the alternative to starving. But the borrower would be culpable of taking advantage of their misfortune. Such taking advantage is the essence of exploitation.[43]

Commentators suggest that such a context for loans helps explain Aquinas' basic argument against lending at interest. He understands lending money to be like lending corn or wine. The wine or corn is consumed as it is used. To charge for both the wine or corn and the use of it would be to charge for two things that are really only one thing. Demanding an exact return of what was lent and consumed is justified, but not an additional charge for its use. Money is like wine or corn in that it is consumed in its use.

---

[43] Wertheimer, 10.

Aquinas distinguishes lending something that is consumed in its use from charging for something not consumed in its use—such as a horse or an apartment. Since neither the horse nor the apartment is consumed as it is used, one may charge for its use and receive the horse or apartment back after the loan (rental) period. The obvious reply to this argument is that sometimes money's use can be distinguished from its consumption: money borrowed to invest is put to work (like a horse). Charging interest for such loan would be permitted according to the logic of Aquinas' argument.

Aquinas himself blocks this argument by appealing to Aristotle's claim that the essence of money is to serve as medium of exchange. Money used for exchange is "consumed in its use." I pay $29.95 in money for the *Critique of Pure Reason* and at the end of the transaction I have the book costing $29.95 and Amazon.com has the $29.95. The money served to make this exchange possible. Without the medium of money, I would need to find a bookseller who wanted to trade the *Critique* for my $29.95 worth of bread or wine (or whatever I had to trade).[44]

Aquinas takes money to have an unalterable intrinsic nature as medium of exchange, and nothing else. He also takes the value of money to be the value established by whoever created it. Thus a $1 bill today and a $1 bill next year and a $1 bill twenty years from now has the same constant value. Of course as soon as one observes that the value of money is what it can buy in the way of goods, and attends to inflation (or deflation), then money's value is not intrinsic, but highly dependent on extrinsic factors.[45]

Aquinas himself comments that coins can sometimes have an additional use beyond facilitating exchange. Thus a coin collector could charge for lending his collection to a museum for exhibition even though he gets it back intact; likewise a bail bondsman who posts bail for an accused person can charge for this service even though when the defendant appears in court he gets his bail money back.[46]

---

[44] *Summa Theologiae* II-II, 78, 1.

[45] Noonan, 395.

[46] *Summa Theologiae* II-II, 78, 1, 6.

Noonan's unsurpassed account of the history of the usury prohibition in scholastic and official church teachings shows how more and more kinds of loans were understood to involve uses of money and other factors (e.g. loss to the lender because of late payment, exchange rate variations, and so forth) that justified taking a payment in addition to the principal. The prohibition on taking interest was thus progressively narrowed to include fewer and fewer kinds of loans. Usury came to mean taking interest on a loan absent one of the many justifying conditions.[47]

The essential point, however, for my inquiry about Aquinas' attitude toward capitalism is that he himself acknowledges the legitimacy of investment for profit. In such cases the lender, while retaining ownership of the money, also bears the risk of loss: "Somebody...who entrusts his money to a merchant or a craftsman in a sort of partnership does not hand over ownership, and so it is still at his risk that the merchant trades or the craftsman works. The lender is, therefore, entitled to ask for a part of the profit of the undertaking in so far as it is his own."[48] Thus the prohibition on taking interest on a loan does not exclude earning profit from the ownership of capital. Such investments are in principle morally permissible. Thus he accepts rather than rejects capitalism's essential feature, profit due to ownership of invested capital.[49]

CONCLUSION

I have argued that Aquinas' economic ethics is not, as Stump claimed, "profoundly anticapitalistic." I have inferred this from what he writes about buying and selling, and investment for profit. Of course, he never treated economic systems as systems, and thus made no explicit judgments about capitalism or socialism, a market economy or a planned economy. His focus, we might say, was "micro," not "macro." It wasn't until the 18th century that the economy as an interconnected system became an object of moral inquiry.

Aquinas' interpretation of prevailing market prices as the measure of just individual acts of selling and buying implies the moral permissibility of free markets. But this is an inference we find relevant to our ques-

---

[47] Noonan, passim.

[48] *Summa Theologiae* II-II, 78, 2, 5.

[49] I am deeply indebted to Noonan for clarifying these issues for me.

tion about the moral assessment of economic systems. Many have taken for granted that a free market system is basically moral. Many of us are comfortable with Aquinas' approval (if only implicit) of this system. We might even claim him as an economic liberal—albeit a paleo- one.

On the other hand, Aquinas is a rigorist about just buying and selling. Unforced mutual agreement, which for many is the measure of just exchange, can be profoundly unjust. The prevailing market price serves as a quasi-objective base line for judging exchanges just or unjust. Thus a party who takes advantage of ignorance or need to obtain a price above (or below) the prevailing market price commits an injustice for which compensation must be made. Aquinas is not original in holding this view. As we have seen the injustice of taking advantage of some one's need or ignorance is commonly referred to as exploitation. Such exploitation is compatible with consent.

Wertheimer illustrates this kind of exploitation by the example of the hardware store owner who after a blizzard sells snow shovels for double their regular price.[50] People who need a snow shovel badly enough will pay the inflated price (no one has a gun to their head). But according to Aquinas' analysis the storeowner acts unjustly in selling shovels for more than the pre-blizzard price and is bound to make restitution. He has taken advantage of customers' special need. No law prohibits exploiting people in this way. But justice does.[51]

Another case of interest in view of Aquinas' position comes from a recent *New York Times Magazine* Ethicist column:

> I occasionally traffic in Persian carpets. A fellow came over about one I'd advertised for $130. He offered $160—evidently he remembered the $175 price of another carpet and was trying to bargain. I accepted, and we each felt we got a great deal. My housemate Dave says, "No harm, no foul." My wife thinks I ripped the guy off. Counsel?[52]

---

[50] Wertheimer, 22.

[51] The general point is clear, but we can easily imagine conditions that muddy the situation. For example, what if the buyer knows what the seller could easily have found out on her own, but hasn't? For a sample of the casuistical questions that the basic norm raises, see, for example, Henry Sidgwick, *Principles of Political Economy*, vol. 2, 580-90.

[52] Randy Cohen, "The Ethicist," *New York Sunday Times Magazine*, Nov. 30, 2003.

Aquinas would agree with the wife. The merchant has taken advantage of the buyer's obvious ignorance of the current advertised price of the carpet. The merchant is bound to make restitution. Alas, "The Ethicist," Randy Cohen, agreed with the housemate.

In sum: Aquinas is not "profoundly anticapitalistic." His analysis of just price assumes the legitimacy of markets in which variations in supply and demand provide opportunities to earn profits from trading. His analysis of the distinction between usury, which is illegitimate, and profits from investments, which are legitimate, assumes that profits from the ownership of capital are morally permissible. We can this infer that he approves, in principle, the essential features of capitalism. However, he insists that this capitalism must be governed by strict moral standards of justice. The capitalism he approves might then turn out to be a capitalism we have never yet seen. But let's not give up hope for building such a moral capitalism, nor renounce it as a norm for judging actually existing capitalisms.

REVIEW ESSAY

THE SPLENDOR OF TRUTH
By Pope John Paul II,
Boston: St. Paul Books, 1993

Reviewed by Alice Ramos
St. John's University

Written in 1993 Pope John Paul II's encyclical *Veritatis Splendor (The Splendor of Truth)* is as relevant today as it was ten years ago. Dealing as it does with the nature of morality, it has attracted the attention of Catholics and non-Catholics, believers and non-believers. For those familiar with the philosophical and theological thought of the present pope, the connection which he establishes in the encyclical between truth and freedom comes as no surprise. This encyclical was in the making for at least five years, and as early as 1986 the Pope referred to the urgent task of grounding ethics in the truth about man and creation. He saw then that it was necessary to base ethical reflection on a true anthropology and this in turn on a metaphysics of creation, which is central to Christian thought (Symposium of Moral Theology, Rome, April 1986). There is certainly in this encyclical an attempt to provide an adequate anthropology, rooted in metaphysical and theological reflection, since for Pope John Paul II only such thought furnishes an answer to the present crisis in ethics. In an attempt to delineate the truth about man, about moral action, and the essential demands of man's personal dignity as the condition for the existence of freedom, the Pope speaks both as the leader of the Catholic Church and as a philosopher-theologian who in his writings prior to the papacy and during the papacy has emphasized the essential relationship which exists between truth, goodness, and freedom.

In this review I would like to concentrate on Pope John Paul II's insistence on the natural law and on the intimate connection between truth and freedom, between law and freedom, which has been traditionally maintained but denied in modern trends of thought in ethics. In speaking in favor of the natural law, the Pope does not intend to impose upon anyone a particular philosophical or theological system (*Veritatis Splendor*, no. 29, p. 45; hereafter cited as *VS*). He is, on the contrary, interested in showing that a proper understanding of the natural law is precisely what harmoniously binds together freedom and nature, for the division and conflict which has arisen between the two is not only dehumanizing man but also destroying him. The question of man's survival, of his very life, was thus in great part the reason for this encyclical on morality.

In an age in which science and technology dominate, in which certitude in matters of morality and religion has become questionable, since only the certitude of mathematical and technical formulae is accepted as reasonable, such a technological view of the world no longer poses the question "Ought we?" but rather concentrates on the question "Can we?", only to respond that what one can do, one should do. With the shift in history and in philosophy from a consideration of man as *homo sapiens* to man as *homo faber*, and thus with the shift from the contemplation of the truth of reality to the domination of nature through action and making processes, man has, to a great extent, ceased to look on nature so as to learn from it, so as to discover and respect its internal laws. Man has thus ceased to read, as it were, the language of nature, to learn from its demands, and to order his actions accordingly. When there is no recourse to the language of human nature, then the first principles of morality which are inscribed in man's rational nature are replaced by the rules of technological and scientific knowledge. As Joseph Cardinal Ratzinger, close collaborator of Pope John Paul II, puts it:

> The good and the moral no longer count, it seems, but only what one can do. . . . And that means . . . that the measure of a human being is what he can do and not what he is, not what is good or bad. What he can do he may do. . . . We should see that the human being can never retreat into the realm of what he is capable of. In everything that he does, he constitutes himself. Therefore he himself, and creation with its good and evil, is always present as his standard, and when he rejects this standard he deceives himself. He does not free himself but places himself in opposition to the truth. And that means that he is destroying himself and the world (*In the Beginning*, (Huntington, Indiana: Our Sunday Visitor, 1990); pp. 85-87).

The fact that total destruction seems to be threatening man and his world is the result of man's own doing, the result of the denial of the truth of his being. Man often lives in a state of perplexity, not knowing who he is, nor where he comes from, nor where he is going. The truth about man and his nature, about moral values, is contested, and thus "freedom alone, uprooted from any objectivity, is left to decide by itself what is good and what is evil" (*VS*, no. 35, pp. 51-52). There is no doubt that we live in an individualistic culture, in which each person faces or makes his own truth, which is different from the truth of others, and where "the individual conscience is accorded the status of a supreme tribunal of moral judgment which hands down categorical and infallible decisions about good and evil" (no. 32, pp. 48-49). Freedom, dissociated from the truth, is thus exalted. And yet, Pope John Paul II tells us that together with this exaltation of freedom, there is also present in modern culture a radical questioning of the very existence of freedom. The studies carried out on the psychological and social conditioning which often influence the exercise of man's freedom have led some to question or even to deny the reality of human freedom.

The affirmation of freedom and its relationship to the truth is, however, crucial to morality. The Pope, in a magnificent conciseness and clarity, says: "Although each individual has a right to be respected in his own journey in search of the truth, there exists a prior moral obligation, and a grave one at that, to seek the truth and to adhere to it once it is known. As Cardinal John Henry Newman, that outstanding defender of the rights of conscience, forcefully put it: 'Conscience has rights because it has duties'" (no. 34, p. 50). Pope John Paul II maintains that man is truly free, that he has dominion over the world and thus shares in God's dominion, and that this dominion extends to man himself. "Just as man in exercising his dominion over the world shapes it in accordance with his own intelligence and will, so too in performing morally good acts, man strengthens, develops and consolidates within himself his likeness to God" (no. 39, p. 55). But what protects and promotes freedom is submission to the natural moral law. Since man is endowed not only with freedom, but also with reason, it is the role of human reason to discover and apply the moral law. And this law does not have its origin in man, but rather in God, in man's Creator. As the Pope says: "The natural law is 'nothing other than the light of understanding infused in us by God, whereby we understand what must be done and what must be avoided. God gave this light and this law to man at creation'" (no. 40, p. 56). Man's practical reason thus participates in the wisdom of the Creator, who is also the ultimate lawgiver; human freedom does not create moral norms. Man's rightful autonomy does not therefore consist in the rejection of the moral law, but rather in the acceptance of the law given by divine wisdom. The growth of human freedom, its perfection, is only possible through obedience to the divine law; "by submitting to the law, freedom submits to the truth of creation," and only such freedom is in conformity with human dignity (nos. 41-42, pp. 57-58). Our freedom is to be subject to that higher reason which is voiced and interpreted by human reason, when our reason rightly distinguishes good from evil. Only in freely doing the good known by right reason, that is, doing the truth, does man reach the Absolute Good and the Absolute Truth, which he desires by nature. By its natural knowledge of God's eternal law, reason is thus able to show man the right direction to take in his free actions (no. 43, p. 59).

The nature of everything that is created by God is ordered to its rightful end through divine wisdom; it is in this way that God cares for his creatures (which is nothing other than divine providence). In the case of man, however, God cares for him not through the laws of physical nature, from without, as it were, but rather from within, through reason (no. 43, p. 59). The Pope quotes from St. Thomas Aquinas's treatise on law in the *Summa Theologiae*: "[The rational creature] has a share of the Eternal Reason, whereby it has a natural inclination to its proper act and end. This participation of the eternal law in the rational creature is called natural law" (ibid.).

Now the conflict which has arisen throughout the history of moral reflection between freedom and law, between freedom and nature, can only be overcome by recognizing the created dimension of nature and understanding its integrity. Physicalist and naturalist objections against the natural law have accused proponents of the traditional conception of natural law of presenting as moral laws what are nothing more than biological laws. Within this way of thinking, a division is created within man himself, for no longer is the human person considered as a unity of body and soul, whose reason and free will are linked to the bodily and sense faculties. The human body becomes devoid of any moral meaning and the person is reduced to a purely formal freedom. In explaining this theory of the human person and of human nature, Pope John Paul II notes that in such a theory: "Human nature and the body appear as *presuppositions or preambles*, materially *necessary*, for freedom to make its choice, yet extrinsic to the person, the subject, and the human act. Their functions would not be able to constitute reference points for moral decisions, because the finalities of these inclinations would be merely 'physical' goods, called by some 'pre-moral'" (no. 48, p. 65). The human person is thus reduced to a freedom which is self-designing, entailing no particular spiritual and bodily structure. In an attempt, therefore, to further explicate the meaning of the natural law, Pope John Paul II insists:

> [The natural law] refers to man's proper and primordial nature, the 'nature of the human person,' which is the *person himself in the unity of soul and body*, in the unity of his spiritual and biological inclinations and of all the other specific characteristics necessary for the pursuit of his end. 'The natural moral law expresses and lays down the purposes, rights and duties which are based upon the bodily and spiritual nature of the human person. Therefore this law cannot be thought of as simply a set of norms on the biological level; rather it must be defined as the rational order whereby man is called by the Creator to direct and regulate his life and actions and in particular to make use of his own body' (no. 50, p. 67).

Thus understood, the natural law does not allow for any division between freedom and nature, but rather links the two intimately together.

Moreover, the Pope asserts that since the natural law is the expression of the truth of man's being, it is "universal in its precepts, and its authority extends to all nations" (no. 51, p. 68). As such, it is also characterized by immutability; although it is true that man lives in a particular culture, his nature is not defined by that culture, since human nature always transcends particular cultures. In recognizing the natural law as the foundation for his fundamental rights and duties, the human person "appropriates the truth of his being and makes it his own by his acts and the corresponding virtues" (no. 52, p. 70). Because of this appropriation or assimilation of the truth contained in the law, there is clearly here no conflict between freedom and law.

When freedom and law are set in oppositionthere arises a "'creative' understanding of moral conscience" (no. 54, p. 73). However, as the Pope says, "Conscience is not an independent and exclusive capacity to decide what is good and what is evil. Rather there is profoundly imprinted upon it a principle of obedience vis-a-vis the objective norm. . . . The truth about moral good, as that truth is declared in the law of reason, is practically and concretely recognized by the judgment of conscience, which leads one to take responsibility for the good or the evil one has done" (no. 61, p. 78). Conscience is presented in such a way that it is not reduced to a merely rigorous observance of universal laws, but rather as a "responsible acceptance of the personal tasks entrusted to man by God" (no. 55, p. 74). Conscience does not merely confront man with the law; it attests rather to man's "faithfulness or unfaithfulness with regard to the law" (no. 57, p. 75). Conscience therefore confronts man not simply with himself, but more importantly, with God, who is the author of the law, the Good and the Truth itself. A mature and responsible conscience thus accepts the law, the truth of man's being, recognizing in that truth man's personal good. The practical judgments of conscience which oblige the person to perform a certain act are, according to the Pope, "not measured by the liberation of the conscience from objective truth, in favor of an alleged autonomy in personal decisions, but, on the contrary, by an insistent search for truth and by allowing oneself to be guided by that truth in one's actions" (no. 61, pp. 78-79). Pope John Paul II's insistence on a search for truth in moral action is in consonance with man's natural desire to know, and man is made not only to know the truth but also to fulfill it in his actions. Only in this way will he arrive at his final end, at happiness, and as the Pope reminds us: "He who does what is true comes to the light" (no. 64, p. 81).

Man's personal good cannot therefore be arrived at through recourse to good intentions or good consequences. An evil act can never be justified by considering the end to which it is directed. Only an act that is in conformity with the authentic, true good can lead man to the light and to eternal life. Man is therefore called to bear witness to the truth in his actions, for only thus will he be authentically free.

Much more can be said of this magnificent document within the framework of divine revelation and faith, but this would lead us further than the confines of this review permit. Let us say, however, that an understanding of the natural law as it is presented here also involves an understanding of man's fundamental orientation to the Absolute Good and the Absolute Truth, that is, God. As Alasdair MacIntyre notes: "In articulating the natural law itself, we understand the peculiar character of our own directedness, and in understanding the natural law better we move initially from what is evident to any plain person's unclouded moral apprehension [that is, a knowledge of God] to what is evident only or at least much more clearly to the *sapientes*, . . ., and to what supernatural revelation discloses" (*Three Rival Versions of Moral Enquiry*, University of Notre Dame Press, 1990; pp. 141-42).

REPORT

"The Human Person and a Culture of Freedom"
University of Chicago & Hyatt Regency, Chicago
October 16-19, 2003
Sponsored by: Pew Forum on Religion and Public Life
Conference Chair: Christopher M. Cullen, S.J., Fordham
University

The Twenty-seventh Annual International Meeting of the American
Maritain Association entitled "The Human Person and a Culture of
Freedom" was held at the University of Chicago & at the Hyatt Regency,
Chicago, Illinois from October 16th to 19th, and was sponsored by the
Pew Forum on Religion and Public Life, and chaired by Christopher M.
Cullen, S.J., of Fordham University.

Given all the concurrent sessions throughout the conference, a person
may, at best, attend about one third to one-half of it. While this is not
advantageous for one who is reporting on it, it is great news for the
Association, and indeed, natural law lovers all over the world. The
Association continues to grow in its resources for natural law scholarship,
in its membership, and in its ability to attract prominent and provocative
speakers. At this conference, for example, Alasdair MacIntyre (Center
for Ethics and Culture, University of Notre Dame) presented a paper on
"Freedom and Punishment," speaking on the idea that causality and
responsibility are not mutually exclusive terms and that there could be
causes (such as moods, dispositions, etc.,) for behavior and, at the same
time, persons being responsible for that behavior; and all of this was in
the concrete and practical context of improving the current prison system
and of answering the question "How do we punish criminals while edu-
cating them for freedom?".

There was Jude Dougherty (Catholic University of America) speaking on "Wretched Aristotle," Jean Bethke Elshtain (University of
Chicago) on "Maritain and Human Rights," Thomas Anderson

(Marquette University) on "Gabriel Marcel on Personal Immortality," Ralph McInerny (University of Notre Dame) on his book *The Very Rich Hours of Jacques Maritain* (University of Notre Dame, 2003), Hadley Arkes (Amherst College) on "The Maladies of the Political Class: When Reasons Cease to Matter," John Deely (University of St. Thomas, Houston) defending his latest work, *Four Ages of Understanding: The First Post-Modern Survey of Philosophy from Ancient Times to the Turn of the Twenty-first Century* (University of Toronto, 2001) before a host of critics, Russell Hittinger (University of Tulsa) on "In Memoriam: Leo XIII (1810-1903): Emergence of the Theme of Freedom in Papal Social Doctrine," James V. Schall, S.J. (Georgetown University) on "The Common Good: Why is it Good? Why is it Common?", Romanus Cessario, O.P., (St. John's Seminary, Boston) on "Freedom and Satisfaction," and Kenneth R. Craycraft, Jr. defending his *The American Myth of Religious Freedom* (Spence Publishing, 1999).

Of all the topics covered in this conference, the one theme that has repeated itself over and over again, is that of the relationship between human freedom and "rights" to divine sovereignty. As it is well known that Aquinas anchors natural law in divine law, the modern world has had to deal with exactly how the relationship between the two gets parsed out. On the issue of rights, for example, should the believer be content with the idea that there are natural rights that may be understood independently of God's creative power and grace or as being firmly situated and understood only within that context? How much does the believer sacrifice or compromise when, in dialogue with the modern world, he or she embraces a secular version of natural rights as did Maritain in his involvement with the United Nations "Universal Declaration of Human Rights"? From Russell Hittinger speaking of the importance of Leo XIII's wish that Thomism "unseat the Rousseauean natural man," to Elshstain's questioning whether one could have human rights without human dignity (to which she answers an ominous "yes") to Kenneth Craycraft arguing that the Lockean Myth is not neutral to the believer, there was the concern for the status of what precisely is "natural" and how this is to be articulated within an adequate metaphysic.

In this conference, the Association is continuing its recent practice of inviting speakers and critics who are really at odds with each other and forced to dialogue. Gone are the days of Thomist scholars preaching to the choir. There are still major fault lines within the current geography of Thomism/Catholic Scholarship and this conference brought them out.

In addition to those speakers already mentioned, there were a few other special treats in this conference. The first was John Deely defending his latest work in the presence of Kenneth Smitz, Curtis Hancock, and Mary C. Sommers. Here the priority of semiotics with regard to metaphysics was questioned and defended especially with regard to *esse* (or existence). While Deely did not see a real difference between His and Gilson's Thomism, Schmitz thought otherwise. Also interesting, and a bit wistful, was Russell Hittinger's tribute to Leo XIII, the Pope that gave a special dignity and mission to Thomists, which has waned in recent years. A special surprise for me was Thomas Anderson (Marquette University), who in a special meeting of the *Gabriel Marcel Society* (which, along with the Etienne Gilson Society, meets regularly at AMA conferences), spoke on "Gabriel Marcel on Personal Immortality." He gave an extremely articulate and Marcellian defense of personal immortality by examining the notion of unconditional love and our ordinary experience of valuing of human persons and how such a love would hardly merit a place in a purely material and death-ridden world.

It was great to see Raymond Dennehy (University of San Francisco) get the "Humanitarian Award," a man who has been on the front lines, as it were, personally defending the sanctity of human life. To cap it off, was Alasdair MacIntyre's gracious acceptance speech for the "Maritain Medal for Scholarly Excellence" award and his exhortation to the American Maritain Association membership, inspiring them about the importance of their work.

There were many more great papers examining, outlining, explicating, debating issues related to Maritain and what he valued. The upcoming volume should prove an extremely valuable resource. Look for this volume with Peter Pagan as the editor.

Among other newsworthy items are this current year's meeting "The Renewal of Civilization: Towards Justice and Peace" in Atlanta, Georgia from October 21rst to the 24th. According to Christopher Cullen, S.J., "We have six excellent plenary session speakers: Elizabeth Fox-Genovese (Emory University), Jorge Garcia (Boston College), Paul Griffiths (University of Illinois at Chicago), Ralph McInerny (University of Notre Dame), Peter Phillips Simpson (City University of New York), and Robert Sokolowski (The Catholic University of America).

Be also sure to explore the most recent titles from the AMA which include: *Truth Matters: Essays in Honor of Jacques Maritain* edited by John G. Trapani Jr., *Faith, Scholarship, and Culture in the 21st Century*, edited by Alice Ramos, and Marie I. George, and *Jacques Maritain and the Many Ways of Knowing*, edited by Douglas A. Ollivant. All of these are distributed by The Catholic University of America Press. For a complete listing of all AMA meetings and publication please see us at our website at http://www.jacquesmaritain.org.

Gregory J. Kerr
DeSales University

BOOK REVIEW

PUBLIC GOODS, PRIVATE GOODS

By Raymond Geuss
Princeton University Press, 2003

Reviewed by Robert L. Chapman
Department of Philosophy & Religious Studies
Pace University, New York

Public Goods, Private Goods was first printed in 2001 in hardback; the second edition paperback reviewed here was brought out in 2003 with one significant change, a new preface. Having read the first edition preface—reprinted in this edition—I must admit its superiority over the 'old' preface. Geuss is quite candid about the rewrite; the editors of first printing (both German and English) requested a nuanced description of his methodology. After reading the book I feel a distinct advantage over those of his first audience.

For some time now Raymond Geuss has been active in criticizing western liberalism, this book is part of that larger enterprise. A central feature of liberalism is the need for a single clear distinction between the public and private realms and the goods associated with each. (Millsian liberalism from which contemporary liberalism receives much of its content begins with the assumption that the distinction between public and private is ontologically real.) Geuss denies such a distinction. (6) His denial is based on a genealogical method of analysis, which turns out to be a "modified" version of a Nietzschean/Foucaultian methodology. (*XVI*) What has been modified is Nietzschean/Foucaultian perspectivism. The defining differences of Geuss' perspectivism' are, he is not interested in examining social institutions, neither is he concerned with uncovering the entanglements of power that promote institutions. He uses a genealogical approach to dissolve the alleged unity of the public/private distinction by examining types of human behavior associated with the distinction from three historical periods.

Examining the past with the hope of finding a necessary connection in meaning and use of concepts between time periods is a fools labor, or so that is what Geuss is out to demonstrate. What you end up with, he claims, is a concretion of disparate beliefs, fragments of ideologies and overlapping contrasts. (10) Left with a series of ramifying assertions must we concede to a non-relative historicism, accept that an accurate history of origin provides no grounds to distinguish between right-wrong, valu-able-valueless offering little insight into the content of the object of inquiry? Yes. Geuss would have it that, "The living past is overwhelm-ingly a realm of gross historical contingency. Any significant human phe-nomena that has succeeded in maintaining itself throughout a long histo-ry into the present, then, can be expected to be a highly stratified com-posite whose parts derive originally from different periods." (*XIII*) (We learn all this from the 'new' preface.)

His argument although not new is refreshing and compelling, and his choice of historical representatives brilliant. Geuss compares the lives of three figures from antiquity from three successive time periods through three types of behavior, and concludes there is no unity of understanding of the public and private distinction: Diogenes of Sinope (shamelessness), Julius Caesar (dignity) and Saint Augustine (love/charitas).

Diogenes is no stranger; founder of the Cynic sect he advanced the position that happiness is attained by satisfying bodily—natural—plea-sures in the least expensive and easiest manner, thus valorizing a life of self-sufficiency (*autapkeia*) Diogenes was notorious for his shameless public behavior: masturbation, urination, defecation and overall lewd-ness. The import of Diogenes' actions was to dramatize the true job of the philosopher, overcoming conventions and social prejudices. As Geuss points out this philosophy-of- life requires complete shamelessness. (27) (Plato, supposedly remarked that Diogenes was 'Socrates gone mad.') (31) From a close look at Diogenes' actions and the Athenians reaction to them, Geuss concludes that although they had no concepts for public and private there are two highly plausible reasons that Diogenes behavior was offensive (as reported by Diogenes Laertius) and from this he draws a dis-tinction between public and private in 4th century Athens (31—33). Public are those spaces we encounter where non-interference is the social norm; private is any space that doesn't admit to non-interference ("principle of disattendability", 32). The distinction itself is not important what are important are the comparisons that follow, for they establish his thesis that distinctions like public and private lack intrinsic connection and historical continuity.

The situation is different when we turn to 1st century Rome where there was an honored distinction between public and private, fittingly expressed by *Res Publica* and *Res Priuatus* and dramatically illustrated by Caesar's conflict with the Senate. As the story goes, by authority of the Roman Senate, Julius Caesar was ordered to resign command of his legions and return to Rome as a private citizen to stand trail for crimes against *res publica*. He refused since such an action would permanently tarnish his reputation (*dignitas*). It is within this context that Geuss stages a multilayered conflict between public and private. As commander of legions, Caesar was a public figure inasmuch as his activities were a concern to all Romans, collectively not distributively (implying a 'common good'). But there is an important sense in which Caesar's dignity is not a matter of the public good, but in all likelihood, a trait necessary for holding a public position in the first place, and although not immune from public validation all the same an attribute earned by personal discipline and thus private.

The interiority of Augustine's spirituality effectively removes the private from social recognition and compliance, placing it squarely in relation to the supernatural. Augustine's inward turn creates an independent ontological place unlike Diogenes' where inattention is suspended, and Caesar's domain for *dignitas* that requires a degree of social recognition. Also, Augustine's 'private' is nearly solipsistic, but for the desirable ongoing redemptive dialogue with God. Public, then, is that which infringes on the conversation between man and God and the stage for disgust and shame only to be overcome by love.

For Diogenes, his public and private share identical ontological status, the only difference between the two is demarcated by where he masturbates, etc.; there is no room for inaccessibility. (Although those witnessing his outlandish actions where offended and would have preferred he conduct such activities in private.) Caesar's private requires external recognition while at the same time is an act of self-interest over and against the "Common good". For Augustine, the private is where one goes to escape the infelicities of a corrupt physical world, accessible only to one's self and God. Geuss rightly insists, from these various conceptions of public/private there is no direct lineage leading to contemporary liberalisms public/private distinction. In fact there is no *the* public/private distinction, only overlapping conflicts. The consequences for liberalism are simple; a new justification for the extensive realm of the private sphere is needed along with a revised history to support it.

CONTRIBUTORS

Polycarp Ikuenobe is an Associate Professor of Philosophy at Kent State University, Kent, Ohio. He obtained his Ph.D. in 1993 from Wayne State University, Detroit, Michigan. He has published a number of articles in his areas of teaching and research interest, which include Philosophy of law, Social and Political Philosophy, African and African-American philosophy, Ethics, Informal Logic, and Critical Thinking. These papers have appeared in such journals as *Journal of Social Philosophy*, *Philosophy East & West*, *Journal of Philosophical Research*, *Vera Lex*, *Journal of Value Inquiry*, *Argumentation*, *Public Affairs Quarterly*, *Metaphilosophy*, *Educational Philosophy and Theory*, *Philosophical Papers*, and *Studies in Philosophy and Education*, among others.

Alice Ramos is Professor of Philosophy at St. John's University in Jamaica, New York. Dr. Ramos holds a Ph.D. in French literature from New York University and a second Ph.D. in Philosophy from the University of Navarra in Pamplona, Spain. She is the recipient of fellowships and grants both here and abroad. She has published a book in Spanish on contemporary semiotics and a metaphysics of the sign, and articles in areas such as Thomistic metaphysics, Kantian ethical theology, contemporary moral inquiry, and Karol Wojtyla-John Paul II's Christian anthropology. She has served as President of the American Maritain Association for three years (2001-2004), and has edited *Beauty, Art, and the Polis* (AMA, 2000; distributed by the CUA Press) and co-edited *Faith, Scholarship, and Culture* in the 21st Century (AMA, 2002; CUA Press). Her present research projects deal with the foundation of ethics and the transcendentals in Thomas Aquinas.

Peter A. Redpath is Professor of Philosophy at St. John's University, Staten Island, N.Y.; executive editor of the Value Inquiry Book Series (VIBS) for the Dutch publisher Editions Rodopi, B.V.; advisor to the philosophy journals *Contemporary Philosophy* and *Man in Culture* (published through the Catholic University of Lublin [KUL], Poland); chairman of the Board of the Angelicum Academy and member of the Board of the Catholic Education Foundation; vice-president and co-founder of the Gilson Society; and former vice-president of the American Maritain Association. He is author/editor of ten books, of many articles in philosophical journals, and lectures extensively nationally and internationally.

Stephen C. Rowntree, SJ, received his Ph.D. in philosophy from Fordham University. His is associate professor of philosophy at Loyola University. After teaching at Loyola from 1976 to 1993, he left to become a founding member of Arrupe College, Harare, Zimbabwe where he taught and helped formed African Jesuit seminarians. In 2001 he returned to Loyola. He recently published, "The Ethics of Trade Policy in Catholic Political Economy," *Theological Studies*, 65 (2004): 596-622.

A small number of back copies of VERA LEX remain at a cost of USD $10.00 a copy.* A complete back set of VERA LEX is $115.00 (see list below). Those who order will receive, without charge, all five previous *graphically reproduced* issues neatly bound: Vol. 1, No. 1 (1979) through Vol. III, No. 1 (1982). [Vol. II No. 2 was not issued.] For more information on Pace titles, please visit the website: *http://www.pace.edu/press*

1982 Vol. III,	No. 2	Reason in the Natural Law
1986 Vol. VI,	No. 1	Edmund Burke and the Natural Law: Theory and Practice
	No. 2	Is There a Natural Law in Hebrew Tradition?
1987 Vol. VII,	No. 1	Natural Law and Constitutionalism
	No. 2	Natural Law and Constitutionalism II
1988 Vol. VIII,	No. 1	Rights I
	No. 2	Rights II
1989 Vol. IX,	No. 1	(General Interest)
	No. 2	The Spanish Tradition (Index: Yves R. Simon)
1990 Vol. X,	No. 1	Thomas Aquinas
	No. 2	(General Interest)
1991 Vol. XI,	No. 1	Equity as Natural Law
	No. 2	Sacred and Secular Natural Law
1992 Vol. XII,	No. 1	Jurisprudence and the Natural Law
	No. 2	Legal Positivism, Pragmatism

1993 Vol. XIII,   **Dignity as Natural Law**
Nos. 1&2 (double issue) (Rosmini, Trigeaud)

1994 Vol. XIV,   **Empirical Natural Law, Human Nature, Science**
Nos. 1&2 (double issue)

1995 Vol. XV,   **Autonomy, Independence, Liberty**
Nos. 1&2 (double issue) (Includes 6-year cumulative index: 1990-1995)

2000 New Series Vol I   **Natural Law and Natural Environment**
Nos. 1&2 (double issue)   (available direct from Pace UP)

2001 New Series Vol. II   **Liberalism and Natural Law**
Nos. 1&2 (double issue)   (available direct from Pace UP)

2002 New Series Vol. III   **Globalism and Natural Law**
Nos. 1&2 (double issue)   (available direct from Pace UP)

*Two back issues of VERA LEX are out of print. However, the originals are available in <u>xeroxed</u> form for USD $5.00.

1983-84 Vol. IV,   **Hugo Grotius** (index)
Nos. 1&2 (double issue)

1985 Vol. V No. 1   **Giambattista Vico**
(No. 2 was not issued.)

Environmental Values

EDITOR:
Alan Holland
Dept. of Philosophy, Furness Coll.,
Lancaster University, LA1 1YG, UK

ASSOCIATED EDITORS:
Michael Hammond
Lancaster University
Robin Grove-White
Lancaster University
John Proops
University of Keele

REVIEWS EDITORS:
Clive Spash
University of Cambridge
Jeremy Roxbee-Cox
Lancaster University

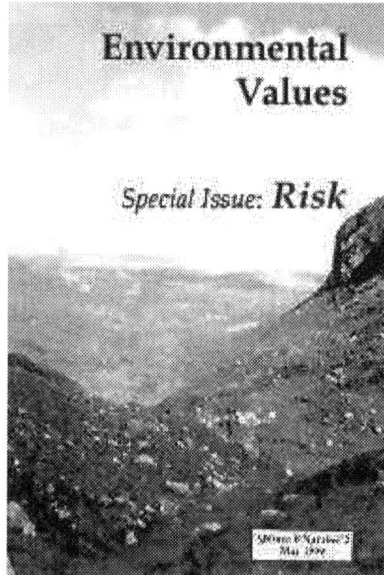

Environmental
Values

Special Issue: *Risk*

ENVIRONMENTAL VALUES is concerned with the basis and justification of environmental policy. It aims to bring together contributions from philosophy, law, economics and other disciplines, which relate to the present and future environment of humans and other species; and to clarify the relationship between practical policy issues and more-fundamental underlying principles or assumptions.

The White Horse Press, 10 High Street, Knapwell, Cambridge CB3 8NR, UK
ISSN: 0963-2719 Quarterly (February, May, August, November)
Vol. 9, 2000, 144 pages per issue. Includes annual index.

Institutions: (1 year) £96 ($155 US)

(Institutional Rate Includes ELECTRONIC ACCESS)

Individual (1 year) £40 ($65 US)

Student/unwaged (1year) £30 ($50 US)

Official Journal of the International Association for
Environmental Philosophy

Environmental Philosophy

$40 ($25 for students) annually with membership to International
Association for Environmental Philosophy

$25 individual non-membership subscription

Send payment to:
Kenneth Maly
Department of Philosophy
University of Wisconsin-LaCrosse,
LaCrosse, WI 54601

Published by the International Association for Environmental Philosophy, the University
of Wisconsin-LaCrosse and the Division of the Environment, University of Toronto

www.ingramcontent.com/pod-product-compliance
Lightning Source LLC
Chambersburg PA
CBHW021601210326
41599CB00010B/552